AF608096

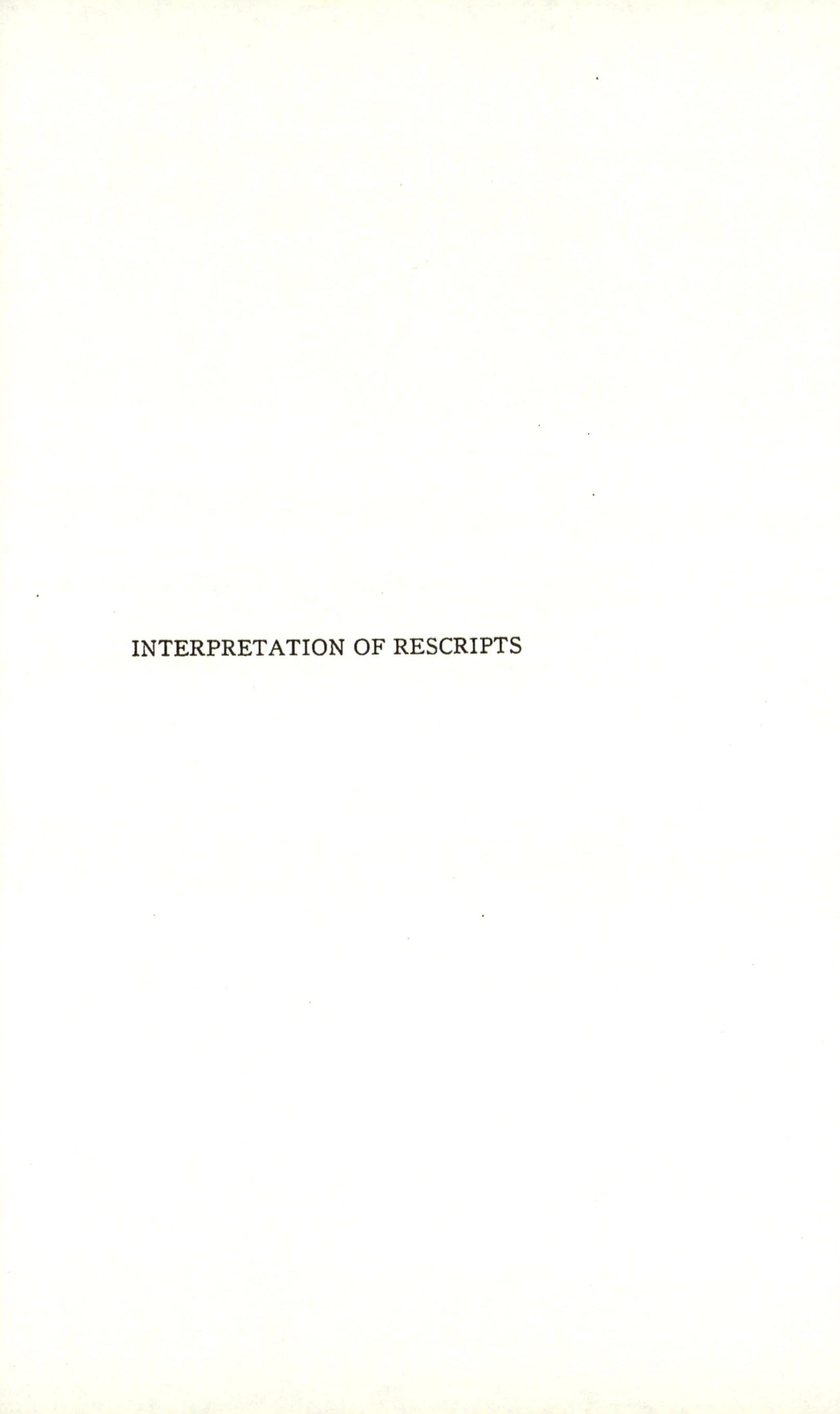

INTERPRETATION OF RESCRIPTS

The writing of this dissertation was conducted under the direction of the Very Rev. John Rogg Schmidt, LL.B., J.C.D., as major professor, and was approved by the Rev. Romaeus W. O'Brien, O.Carm., J.C.D., and the Rev. Frederick R. McManus, J.C.D., as readers.

THE CATHOLIC UNIVERSITY OF AMERICA
CANON LAW STUDIES
No. 398

Interpretation of Rescripts

A Commentary with Historical Notes

A DISSERTATION

SUBMITTED TO THE FACULTY OF THE SCHOOL OF CANON LAW OF THE CATHOLIC UNIVERSITY OF AMERICA IN PARTIAL FULFILLMENT OF THE REQUIREMENTS FOR THE DEGREE OF DOCTOR OF CANON LAW

BY THE
REV. BERNARD C. GERHARDT, J.C.L.
PRIEST OF THE ARCHDIOCESE OF WASHINGTON

THE CATHOLIC UNIVERSITY OF AMERICA PRESS
WASHINGTON, D. C.
1959

NIHIL OBSTAT:

JOANNES R. SCHMIDT, LL.B., J.C.D.

Censor Deputatus

Washingtonii, die 21 novembris, 1958

IMPRIMATUR:

✠ PATRICIUS A. O'BOYLE, D.D.

Archiepiscopus Washingtonensis

Washingtonii, die 24 novembris, 1958

MURRAY AND HEISTER, INC.
WASHINGTON, D. C.

PRINTED BY
TIMES AND NEWS PUBLISHING CO.
GETTYSBURG, PA., U. S. A.

FOREWORD

From the very early days of the Church, rescripts have been used as one of the chief means of expediting ecclesiastical affairs. They continue to be used in ever increasing numbers as the organization of the Church expands and grows. Written replies are constantly being issued by the Holy See, as well as subordinate ecclesiastical superiors, in answer to the numerous requests and petitions that are directed to them. It is important, therefore, that these replies be correctly understood by those who petition, receive and put them to use.

Ordinarily, the words of a rescript will be clear enough that they will need no explanation. It is to be expected that the ecclesiastical superior who issues a rescript will make every reasonable effort to be clearly understood. Since it is not always possible to express one's thoughts in perfectly clear language, or to express or explain the implications of legal terminology and content, there will be times when the terms of a rescript will require some further explanation. It will be necessary, then, to interpret the rescript.

The Code of Canon Law contains the various juridic norms which govern the interpretation of rescripts. The present study is devoted to a commentary on these norms, together with historical notations which serve to point out the legal sources from which the rules have developed and their significance for the norms themselves. There are three parts to this treatise. In the first part there is an explanation of the notions and divisions of interpretation and of rescripts. The second part is concerned with the general norms for the interpretation of rescripts. The third part treats of the special norms for their interpretation.

The writer welcomes this occasion to thank His Excellency, the Most Reverend Patrick A. O'Boyle, D.D., Archbishop of Washington, for the opportunity of graduate study in Canon Law at the Catholic University of America. He also wishes to thank the members of the Faculty of the School of Canon Law, his classmates at the University and all those who have helped in the preparation of this dissertation.

TABLE OF CONTENTS

TABLE OF CONTENTS (Continued)

TABLE OF CONTENTS (Continued)

PART III

The Special Norms for the Interpretation of Rescripts

PART I

Preliminary Considerations

CHAPTER I

The Notion and Divisions of Interpretation

Before considering the principles which govern the interpretation of rescripts, a few preliminary considerations regarding interpretation in general are in order. The present chapter will be concerned with various aspects of interpretation, but its principal purpose will be to clarify somewhat the diversified terminology used by authors to express the notion and divisions of interpretation.

The major portion of canonical literature on the subject of interpretation is found in connection with the discussion, by various authors, of the question of the interpretation of law. Hence, the general notion and division of the interpretation of law as developed by the authors, both before and after the Code of Canon Law, will form the basis for the material to follow.

The principles governing the interpretation of rescripts are but applications, with proper modifications, of the general rules for the interpretation of law.[1] The legal terminology encountered in research on the interpretation of law and the interpretation of rescripts is fundamentally the same. The authors more or less take for granted the terminology when considering rescripts. They discuss it more fully in connection with the interpretation of law. For that reason also, the emphasis in the present chapter will be on law rather than on rescripts as such.

ARTICLE I. THE GENERAL NOTION OF INTERPRETATION

Interpretation, in general, may be defined as the explanation or declaration of the meaning of a word, a phrase, a sentence or any such combination of words.[2] Ordinarily, interpretation supposes

[1] Michiels, *Normae Generales Juris Canonici* (2. ed., 2 vols., Parisiis-Tornaci-Romae: Desclée et Socii, 1949), II, 422 (hereafter cited *Normae Generales*).

[2] "Interpretatio generatim aliud non est quam congrua verbi, vel sententiae, per aliud clarius explicatio."—Reiffenstuel (1642-1703), *Jus Canonicum Universum* (5 vols. in 7, Parisiis, 1864-1870), Lib. I, tit. II, n. 351; cf. also Michiels, *Normae Generales,* I, 471.

a doubt, for where the meaning of a word or phrase is clear there will be no need for an explanation or declaration of what the word or phrase signifies.[3] Its principal effect is to render a doubtful expression clear and certain.

Due to the limitations of the human intellect, not only is it difficult at times to form clear ideas, it is often more arduous to find the proper words to give clear expression to these ideas. In legal matters, where it is often necessary for the legislator to make known his intention in concise legal terminology, this difficulty is thereby increased.[4]

In the interpretation of a law or any legal document, such as a rescript, the doubt which occasions the need of interpretation may concern the meaning of the words used. Even where the meaning of the words is clear, there may be doubt as to whether the intention of their author is other than the words would indicate. Then again, one may doubt whether a particular person, case or thing is to be included within the otherwise clear meaning of the words. Thus, the doubt may have as its object the meaning of the words, the intention of their author, or the application of his words to a concrete case.[5]

The purpose of interpretation in law is to discover the will or intention of the legislator. The chief means for arriving at a knowledge of what the legislator intends or wishes are the words which he uses.[6] In formulating the definition and divisions of inter-

---

[3] "Interpretatio est verbi, vel sententiae obscurae per aliud declaratio."—Laymann (1574-1635), *Theologia Moralis* (Venetiis, 1630), Lib. I, tract. IV, cap. XVIII, n. 1; cf. also Brems, "De Interpretatione Authentica Codicis J. C. per Pont. Commissionem," *Jus Pontificium* (Romae, 1921-1940), XV (1935), 164.

[4] "Haec est humana conditio, ut vix possit homo tam perspicuis verbis sensum suum explicare, quin ambiguitates ac dubia nascantur."—Suarez (1548-1617), *De Legibus ac Deo Legislatore, Libri Decem,—Opera Omnia* (26 vols. in 23, editio nova a Carolo Berton, Parisiis: apud Ludovicum Vives, 1856-1868), lib. VI, c. 1, n. 5 (hereafter cited *De Legibus*).

[5] Brems, *art. cit.,* pp. 169-171.

[6] Cf. Michiels, *Normae Generales,* I, 472-473; cf. also White, *The Evolution of the Canonical Concept of Strict Interpretation of Law* (Excerpta ex Dissertatione ad Lauream, Romae: Pontificia Universitas Gregoriana, 1952), p. 11.

pretation some authors emphasize the meaning of the words, while others seem to concentrate more on the will or intention of the legislator. This emphasis on one or the other aspect of interpretation is the chief cause for the diversity of terminology among them.

Suarez, for instance, states that the interpretation of law consists in the expression and understanding of the immediate and proper sense of the law itself based on the proper meaning of the words.[7]

Wernz more or less repeats the first part of Suarez' definition. According to him, interpretation is the explanation of the sense contained in a law from the beginning.[8] Later on in his discussion of interpretation, he remarks that only the explanation of a doubtful or obscure law according to the proper meaning of words is interpretation in the true sense.[9]

One group of contemporary writers, following the example of Wernz, defines interpretation in brief terms as the explanation, or manifestation, of the meaning of a law.[10] A second group defines it as the explanation of the meaning of the law according to the mind of the legislator.[11] Beste includes both ideas in his definition.[12] Still

---

[7] "Legis interpretatio, si praecise ac secundum vocis rigorem sumatur, solum consistit, in declaratione et intelligentia proprii et (ut sic dicam) immediati sensus ipsius legis, sistendo tantum in usitata et propria significatione verborum et in sensu legis ex illis sic intellectis resultante. . . ."—*De Legibus,* lib. VI, c. II, n. 1.

[8] "Interpretatio generatim est explicatio (manifestatio, vel significatio) sensus in lege lata ab initio iam contenti sive comprehensi."—*Ius Decretalium,* I (3. ed., Prati, 1913), n. 127.

[9] *Ibid.,* n. 128 ad II.

[10] Cf. Cappello, *Summa Iuris Canonici* (4. ed., 3 vols., Romae: Aedes Universitatis Gregorianae, 1945-1955), I, 66; Vermeersch-Creusen, *Epitome Iuris Canonici cum Commentariis ad Scholas et ad Usum Privatum* (3 vols., Vol. I, 7. ed., 1949; Vol. II, 6. ed., 1940; Vol. III, 6. ed., 1946, Mechliniae-Romae: H. Dessain), I, n. 39 (hereafter cited *Epitome*); Van Hove, *Commentarium Lovaniense* I, Tom. I (*De Legibus Ecclesiasticis*) (Mechliniae, 1930), n. 239 (hereafter cited *De Legibus*).

[11] Cf. Abbo-Hannan, *The Sacred Canons* (2 vols., St. Louis: B. Herder Book Co., 1952), I, 31; Coronata, *Institutiones Iuris Canonici* (4. ed., 5 vols., Taurini-Romae: Marietti, 1947-1951), I, n. 22 (hereafter cited *Institutiones*); Maroto, *Institutiones Iuris Canonici* (2 vols., Madrid, 1919), I, n. 236 (hereafter cited *Institutiones*).

[12] "*Interpretatio* est aperitio sensus in lege contenti, seu, paulo explicatius, est indagatio et manifestatio (*ex-plicatio*) voluntatis, quam legislator in actu

another group defines interpretation as the explanation of the true meaning of the law.[13]

Michiels takes exception to Suarez' definition of interpretation as quoted above. He contends that to interpret a law is to explain the true meaning of the law as intended by the legislator. For him, Suarez' definition does not go far enough. While the proper meaning of words ordinarily conveys the intention of the legislator, this is not always the case, and, therefore, it is necessary to determine the *true* meaning of the words.[14]

Michiels maintains that the proper object of interpretation is the will of the legislator as expressed in the verbal formula which he uses. To ascertain the will of the legislator, it is necessary to investigate and discover the meaning of the words which he uses to make known his intention. Since the verbal formula used by the legislator constitutes the law, in so far as it really conveys his legislative intent, the important thing is to determine the *real,* or *true,* meaning of the words. The real meaning of the words is the meaning actually intended by the legislator. Ordinarily, the legislator uses words in their proper meaning, and hence, the proper meaning of the words will usually be the one which he actually intends. However, the rule is not absolute, according to Michiels, for there are times when the legislator will depart from the proper meaning of words and use them in an improper sense. It is the function of the interpreter, then, to examine and find out what is the actual meaning intended by the legislator.[15]

---

formationis legis de facto habuit, verbis suis alligavit et in formula legis conditae protulit."—*Introductio in Codicem* (3. ed., Collegeville, Minn.: St. John's Abbey Press, 1946), p. 76.

[13] Cicognani, *Canon Law* (2. ed., authorized English version by Joseph M. O'Hara and Francis J. Brennan, Philadelphia: The Dolphin Press, 1935), p. 598; Michiels, *Normae Generales,* I, 473, 474.

[14] *Ibid.,* p. 476, note 1. In making his point, Michiels cites Ferraris (+ 1763) and gives almost a verbatim repetition of the latter's notion of interpretation. According to Ferraris, "Interpretatio autem nihil aliud est quam congrua per aliud clarius explicatio verborum Legis ordinata ad concipiendum verum Legis sensum a Legislatore intentum. . . ."—*Prompta Bibliotheca, Canonica, Iuridica, Moralis, Theologica, necnon Ascetica, Polemica, Rubricistica, Historica* (ed. novissima, 9 vols., Romae, 1885-1889), V, "Lex," art. V, n. 18 (hereafter cited *Prompta Bibliotheca*).

[15] *Ibid.,* pp. 472-475.

It is not the purpose of the present article to settle the differences among authors regarding the notion of interpretation of law. Rather, its aim is to familiarize the reader with the general notion of interpretation in preparation for the discussion of the interpretation of rescripts. Interpretation alone may be considered as the explanation of the meaning of a word. Applied to law, it is variously defined by authors as the explanation of the meaning of a law; the explanation of the meaning of a law according to the proper meaning of the words; the explanation of the meaning of a law according to the mind of the legislator; and finally, the explanation of the meaning of a law according to the true sense of the words. The term "rescript" could be substituted for the term "law" in any of the above definitions. Instead of defining the interpretation of rescripts at this time, it would be well to consider the various divisions of interpretation as outlined in the authors.

ARTICLE II. THE DIVISIONS OF INTERPRETATION

In treating of the interpretation of law, authors usually follow their discussion of the notion of interpretation by listing the various divisions of interpretation. They group the divisions within three general categories, and in the first category, they consider interpretation according to its source or author. In the second, they divide interpretation according to its effect. In the third, they list the means used, or the manner in which interpretation is made.

It will not be necessary to dwell at length on all of these divisions. Those of the second category will be considered more fully than the others, for they will be referred to repeatedly in regard to the interpretation of rescripts.

Section 1. Author of Interpretation

By reason of its source or author, interpretation is authentic, doctrinal or customary. This is a division made popular by canonists both before and after the Code.[16] Of more immediate concern

---

[16] Among pre-Code authors cf. Suarez, *De Legibus,* lib. VI, c. 1, n. 1; Reiffenstuel, *Jus Canonicum Universum,* lib. I, tit. II, nn. 357-364. Of those after the Code cf. Michiels, *Normae Generales,* I, 482, 483; Van Hove, *De Legibus,* n. 242.

here are authentic and doctrinal interpretation, although mention will be made of custom as a source of interpretation.

Authentic interpretation differs from that which is doctrinal in two ways in particular. First of all, the two differ according to the authority of the one who issues the interpretation. Authentic interpretation is given by one who has official or public authority to do so. For that reason, it is sometimes referred to as authoritative interpretation.[17] The authentic interpreter may be the legislator himself, his successor in office or one to whom either has committed the power of interpretation.[18] For the universal Church, the legislator is the Supreme Pontiff or an ecumenical council; for several provinces together, the plenary council; for one province, the provincial council; for a diocese, the Bishop either in synod or outside of a synod. For a vacant see, the Vicar Capitular is the legislator. However, where chapters do not exist, the Administrator appointed by the diocesan consultors has legislative power. The power of authentic interpretation may be given to another by any one of the above-mentioned legislators. As an example, mention may be made of the Pontifical Commission for the Authentic Interpretation of the Canons of the Code of Canon Law, created by Benedict XV in his Motu proprio, "Cum iuris canonici," of September 15, 1917.[19]

Authentic interpretation also differs from doctrinal interpretation by reason of its binding force, or the manner in which it obliges those for whom it is given. It is compulsory in the sense that it must be complied with and must be adhered to by those who are subject to it. Depending on the way in which it is given, authentic interpre-

---

[17] Bouscaren-Ellis, *Canon Law, A Text and Commentary* (Milwaukee: The Bruce Publishing Co., 1946: Reprint, 1948), p. 31 (hereafter cited *Canon Law*); Wernz, *Ius Decretalium,* I, n. 128. For a complete treatment of authentic interpretation, cf. Schmidt, *The Principles of Authentic Interpretation in Canon 17 of the Code of Canon Law,* The Catholic University of America Canon Law Studies, n. 141 (Washington, D. C.: The Catholic University of America Press, 1941) (hereafter cited *The Principles of Authentic Interpretation*); cf. also Brems, "De Interpretatione Authentica Codicis J. C. Per Pont. Commissionem," *Jus Pontificium* (Romae, 1921-1940), XV (1935), 161-190, 298-313; XVI (1936), 78-105, 217-256.

[18] Can. 17, § 1.

[19] *Acta Apostolicae Sedis* (Romae, 1909-), IX (1917), 483-484.

tation may be one of two kinds. If it is issued in the form of a law, it has the force of the law which it interprets and obliges all those who are subject to the law.[20] This form of interpretation is often referred to as general authentic interpretation. If the interpretation is given in the form of a particular application of the law through a rescript, or by way of a judicial sentence, it does not have the force of a law. However, it does bind the parties for whom it is issued and directly affects the things concerning which the sentence is passed or the rescript granted.[21] It is therefore called particular authentic interpretation.[22]

Doctrinal interpretation does not proceed from one having public authority, nor does it *per se* have the binding force of law. Instead, it proceeds from those learned in the law, i.e., from the opinions of renowned canonists. It is given privately by one who knows the law. Of itself, a doctrinal interpretation induces no obligation, but only represents a private opinion. Its binding force depends upon the value of the juridic reasoning which supports it. However, where canonists are in agreement concerning a particular interpretation, the fact that they agree lends weight to their opinion and can produce moral certitude as to the correctness of their interpretation.[23]

The Code of Canon Law makes no attempt to define doctrinal interpretation. It does, however, indicate the norms which are to be followed in this form of interpretation. Canons 18 and 19 set forth the principles which govern the doctrinal interpretation of law, while canons 49 and 50 contain similar rules for the interpretation of rescripts.

Interpretation that is customary, or according to usage, proceeds from the common observance of a law or from a custom legitimately introduced in a community. It is not obligatory as long as the legal prescriptions for custom are not fulfilled. Once the canonical requirements are fulfilled, however, a juridic custom is introduced

---

[20] Can. 17, § 2.

[21] Can. 17, § 3.

[22] Cf. Cicognani, *Canon Law*, pp. 601-603; Schmidt, *op. cit.*, pp. 107-117, 273-276.

[23] Brys, *Tractatus De Legibus* (Brugis: Car. Beyaert, 1942), p. 85; Schmidt, *op. cit.*, p. 131, note 46; Van Hove, *De Legibus*, n. 242.

and has the force of law. Until then, custom or usage can serve as a norm for interpretation without enjoying obligatory force.[24]

Section 2. Effects of Interpretation

Interpretation may have various effects, depending upon whether it states in clearer terms what is not doubtful, explains what is really doubtful, restricts or extends the meaning of words or uses words in a strict or broad sense. Authors use a great variety of terms to denote the different effects of interpretation, so many in fact, that it is necessary to examine each author carefully to determine the precise sense of the terms that he uses. The principal purpose of this section will be to outline the effects of interpretation. It will serve at the same time to familiarize the reader with the terminology employed by authors when discussing the interpretation of rescripts as well as the interpretation of law.

There will be three subdivisions within this section. The first will consider declaratory and explanatory interpretation. The second will be concerned mainly with restrictive and extensive interpretation, as well as several variations or refinements of the two concepts as made by a number of canonists. The third subdivision will treat of strict and broad interpretation.

A. Declarative and Explanatory Interpretation

The principal difference between interpretation that is *merely declarative* and that which is *explanatory* is that the former merely restates in clearer terms the meaning of words that are clear in themselves, while the latter explains words that are in themselves doubtful. The distinction between the two types of interpretation is not a new one. Evidence of it is found in decretal law. Nicholas III (1277-1280), for example, in his constitution, *"Exiit qui seminat,"* ordered that the constitution should be understood as it was given and forbade anything more than a restatement of the law in more intelligible terms.[25]

---

[24] Beste, *Introductio in Codicem,* p. 77; Michiels, *Normae Generales,* I, 483; cf. cans. 25-30.

[25] The law prescribed *versus finem*: ". . . ut praesens constitutio, cum ipsam legi contigerit, sicut prolata est, sic fideliter exponatur ad literam,

Among the decretalists, the term *"declaratio"* and the expression *"interpretatio declarativa"* are used to denote the explanation of a doubtful law, as well as the exposition of a law where there is no mention of a doubt. At times, they include what the authors refer to as *interpretatio translativa vel linguarum,* which seems to amount to no more than a translation or definition of terms. In general, all that can be said of these earlier writers is that, for them, the term *"declaratio"* includes the *declaratio* of even a doubtful law as well as the *interpretatio translativa,* and that the line of demarcation between the two is not clearly marked.[26] The main difficulty in reading the early authors, then, is that, while they understand the difference between interpretation which is now referred to as merely declarative and interpretation that is explanatory, they use the same term in denoting both.

For Suarez, declarative interpretation consists in the expression and understanding of the immediate and proper sense of the law itself, based on the proper meaning of the words. He makes no mention of doubt in connection with this form of interpretation, and, for him, it would seem to be no more than a restatement of the law itself.[27]

Reiffenstuel, however, has more to say on the subject. According to him, declarative interpretation, or *interpretatio litteralis* as he also refers to it, is had when the words of a law are explained through the use of clearer words. He states that *declaratio* is not interpretation in the strict sense, since it merely explains what is contained in the words of the law. It is concerned mainly with the words of a law and offers nothing new, but only makes clearer what is comprehended by these words.[28]

---

concordantiae, contrarietates seu diversae vel adversae opiniones a lectoribus seu expositoribus nullatenus inducantur. Super ipsa constitutione glossae non fiant, nisi forsan, per quas verbum vel verbi sensus, seu constructio, vel ipsa constructio quasi grammaticaliter ad literam vel intelligibilius exponatur."—C. 3, *de verborum significatione,* V, 12 in VI; Potthast, *Regesta Pontificum Romanorum inde ab anno post Christum natum* 1198 *ad annum* 1304 (2 vols., Berolini, 1874-1875), n. 21629 (hereafter cited Potthast).

[26] Cf. Schmidt, *op. cit.,* p. 134, note 59; p. 135, note 62.

[27] *De Legibus,* lib. VI, c. 2, n. 1; cf. White, *op. cit.,* pp. 11, 12.

[28] *Jus Canonicum Universum,* lib. I, tit. 11, nn. 351, 352; cf. also White, *op. cit.,* p. 28.

Regarding the interpretation of a doubtful law, Reiffenstuel is not too clear as far as terminology is concerned. In one place, he seems to include it under the heading of declarative interpretation. He mentions that interpretation is declarative when one either declares the sense of a law or interprets its doubtful words.[29] Elsewhere, he considers a doubtful law in connection with what he refers to as interpretation in the proper sense, or *interpretatio per modum suppletionis*. Such interpretation, according to him, seeks to determine the mind of the law and is accompanied by an at least initial departure from its words.[30] It would seem, then, to be more than a mere explanation of doubtful words, and will be discussed more fully in the subdivision which follows.

Writing toward the middle of the eighteenth century, Ferraris describes declarative interpretation as a suitable exposition of doubtful and obscure words.[31] His contemporary, Böckhn (1690-1752), gives a similar description, and adds that declarative interpretation is to be used only when words are obscure, and not if a law is clear.[32]

Later authors prior to the Code tend to differentiate more adequately between declarative and explanatory interpretation. However, they also begin to use the expression "comprehensive interpretation" to denote either, or both, of the foregoing, i.e., declarative and explanatory interpretation. Thus, in one respect, they help to clarify the use of terms, but, at the same time, they confuse the notion of comprehensive interpretation as it had been understood up to that time.[33]

Wernz distinguishes between interpretation in the broad sense and interpretation in the strict sense. He states that the exposition of the meaning of the words of a law that are clear in themselves, through the use of clearer words, is to be considered as interpreta-

---

[29] *Ibid.*, n. 367.

[30] *Ibid.*, nn. 352, 353.

[31] *Prompta Bibliotheca,* V, "Lex," art. V, n. 20.

[32] *Commentarium in Jus Canonicum* (3 vols., Salisburgi, et invenitur Parisiis, 1776), Tom. I, lib. I, tit. II, § 7, nn. 122, 123 (hereafter cited *Commentarium*).

[33] Cf. Brems, "De Interpretatione Authentica Codicis J. C. per Pont. Commissionem," *Jus Pontificium,* XV (1935), 173.

tion in the broad sense. He mentions the fact that, among the earlier authors, this form of interpretation was called *declaratio* and, at times, specifically referred to as *comprehensiva.* Wernz himself, however, does not actually call it declarative interpretation. As opposed to interpretation in the broad sense, he points out that in the strict sense interpretation is the explanation of the doubtful or obscure meaning of the law.[34]

From the discussion of declarative and explanatory interpretation up to this point, it is evident that, in the jurisprudence of the authors prior to the Code, *declaratio,* or *interpretatio declarativa,* includes more than a mere restatement of clear terms. As will be seen immediately, it is not to be identified with the concept of merely declarative interpretation as contained in canon 17, § 2. It goes beyond that concept and includes all interpretation that is not extensive or restrictive.[35]

Although the Code of Canon Law does not deal *ex professo* with the notion and divisions of interpretation, it does clearly distinguish between interpretation that is merely declarative and interpretation that explains a doubtful law. It considers both as divisions of authentic interpretation given in the form of a law. It avoids naming any divisions as such, as if to bypass the controversies which were occasioned by the use of such terms as *declarativa,* or *comprehensiva.* Instead, canon 17, § 2 states directly that, if authentic interpretation merely declares the meaning of the words of a law that are clear in themselves, the interpretation need not be promulgated, and it has retroactive effect. If it explains a doubtful law, such interpretation does not have retroactive effect and must be promulgated.

Since the Code does not determine the divisions of interpretation as such, modern authors still use a variety of terms in discussing its various effects. With regard to interpretation that merely declares the meaning of words that are clear in themselves the terminology is more or less uniform. When treating of this species of interpretation, the majority of canonists refer to it as

---

[34] *Ius Decretalium,* I, n. 127.

[35] Cf. Schmidt, *The Principles of Authentic Interpretation,* p. 138.

declarative, or merely declarative interpretation.[36] With regard to interpretation that explains a doubtful law, a good number of canonists describe it as explanatory (*explicativa*).[37] For Cicognani, it is declarative interpretation properly so-called.[38] Others use the term "comprehensive" in reference to it.[39] Several authors call declarative interpretation *declaratio legis* and consider explanatory interpretation as interpretation in the proper sense.[40] Although, theoretically, this terminology may be correct, it has not found favor among canonists since the Code. The main reason is the fact that the Code, itself, includes both as forms of authentic interpretation.[41] Strictly speaking, interpretation is necessary only where there is doubt. However, from the practical standpoint, the declaration or exposition of the meaning of words that are clear in themselves amounts to an interpretation, and is considered as much by the Code in canon 17, § 2. Therefore, it is preferable to refer to both declarative and explanatory interpretation as interpretation in the proper sense. Following the example of Wernz, the former is to be thought of as interpretation in the broad sense, and the latter as interpretation in the strict sense.[42]

Despite the diversity of terminology they use in designating it, authors, in general, agree as to the fundamental notion of declarative interpretation in the sense of Canon 17, § 2. Following the Code, they define it as interpretation which merely declares the meaning of words that are clear in themselves. They point out that the words of a law are clear in themselves when there can be no objective doubt as to their meaning. The purpose of declarative interpretation is to remove subjective doubts, or doubts which

[36] Cf. Abbo-Hannan, *The Sacred Canons,* p. 32; Beste, *Introductio in Codicem,* p. 78; Coronata, *Institutiones,* I, n. 22; Michiels, *Normae Generales,* I, 480; Van Hove, *De Legibus,* n. 242.

[37] Cf. Beste, *loc. cit.;* Michiels, *loc. cit.;* Schmidt, *The Principles of Authentic Interpretation,* p. 168.

[38] *Canon Law,* p. 599.

[39] Cf. Abbo-Hannan, *loc. cit.;* Coronata, *loc. cit.*

[40] Cf. Brys, *Tractatus De Legibus,* pp. 84, 85; Cappello, *Summa Iuris Canonici,* p. 66.

[41] Can. 17, § 2.

[42] *Ius Decretalium,* I, n. 127; cf. also Brems, "De Interpretatione Authentica Codicis J. C. Per Pont. Commissionem," *Jus Pontificium,* XV (1935), 180.

arise in the mind of a person through ignorance, inadvertence or failure to take into consideration some circumstance or detail of a law. Such doubts, of themselves, do not render a law uncertain. However, they cause it to be unknown. Hence, there is need for a clearer exposition of terms. Declarative interpretation, in regard to law, then, is a restatement of what is already objectively contained in the law. It restates the law in such a way, that those who had doubts about it are able to understand it clearly.[43]

Canons 18 and 19 of the Code list the rules to be followed in the declarative interpretation of law. Only after the rules have been applied and doubt remains, can a law be said to be objectively doubtful. Their chief purpose is to remove the subjective doubts mentioned in the paragraph above, and thereby to reveal the underlying clarity of the text of the law.[44]

As will be explained in the chapters to follow, canons 49 and 50 offer similar rules for the interpretation of rescripts.[45]

B. Extensive and Restrictive Interpretation

Concerning extension and restriction in law, authors before and after the Code agree as to the fundamental notions of the two types of interpretation. Extensive interpretation broadens the scope of a law, while restrictive interpretation narrows its limits. However, the same authors more or less divide themselves into two opposing groups in discussing the problem of the *terminus a quo*, or the point of departure whence extensive and restrictive interpretation proceed. For one group, the *terminus a quo* is the proper meaning of the words. For the other, it is the mind or intention of the legislator. Thus, for the authors of the first group, interpretation will be extensive when it proceeds beyond the proper meaning of words of a law. For those of the second group, it will be extensive when it goes beyond the mind of the legislator. The difference between the two groups will be seen more clearly in the discussion that follows, in which a brief historical survey of the notions of extensive and restrictive interpretation will be given.

---

[43] Cf. Cicognani, *Canon Law*, pp. 601, 602; Michiels, *Normae Generales*, I, 480; Schmidt, *The Principles of Authentic Interpretation*, p. 118.

[44] Cf. Schmidt, *ibid.*, p. 123.

[45] Chapters III-VII.

Suarez considers at great length the question of the extension of law. For him, it is the fundamental problem of all interpretation. He gives various divisions of extension, depending upon the relation of the notion of extension to the proper meaning of the words of a law. He makes the proper meaning of words, then, the *terminus a quo,* or the point from which extensive interpretation will originate. In the beginning of his discussion, Suarez mentions extension that stays within the proper meaning of words and varies according to whether the natural, common or legal sense of a given word is used. He uses the term "extension" here, but is actually dealing with the concepts of strict and broad interpretation as will be seen in the subdivision of interpretation that follows this one. Regarding extension that goes beyond the proper meaning of words, he makes mention of two types, namely, interpretation that extends the proper meaning of words to an improper sense, and interpretation that goes beyond even the improper meaning of words because of the similarity or identity of the *ratio legis.* In addition, and more or less in passing, he speaks of extension that goes beyond the mind of the legislator. He is quick to point out, however, that such extension cannot be admitted.[46]

Further on, in treating the question of the extension of law beyond the proper meaning of its words by reason of the similarity or identity of the *ratio legis,* Suarez distinguishes between extension that is comprehensive and interpretation which he calls purely extensive. It will not be necessary, at this time, to inquire into the solution which Suarez gives to the question. Of immediate interest are his notions of comprehensive and purely extensive interpretation. The former, according to him, amounts to a broadening of the scope of the law to include a person or case which, while actually an object of the legislator's will, is not well enough expressed in the words of the law.[47] The latter is had when the disposition of the law is extended to a case not actually the object

---

[46] *De Legibus,* lib. VI, c. II, n. 2; cf. White, *The Evolution of the Canonical Concept of Strict Interpretation of Law,* pp. 11, 12.

[47] "Comprehensive interpretatio, vel extensio, est quando per illam declaratur talem casum vel personam comprehensam fuisse in mente legislatoris, licet verbis non satis iam declaraverit . . ."—*op. cit.,* lib. VI, c. III, n. 9; cf. White, *ibid.,* p. 14.

of the will of the legislator because there is a similarity of the reason or purpose of the law.[48]

Suarez allows the extension (comprehensive interpretation) of the provisions of a law to other cases, provided there is real identity of purpose, that is, where the end or purpose of the law is the immediate object of the legislator's will in founding the law. He adds precisely, however, that such extension is comprehensive (in as much as it is not beyond the mind of the legislator). He does not allow this extension of a law to other cases because of a mere similarity of purpose. According to Suarez, this latter interpretation would be pure extension (beyond the mind of the legislator). For him, pure extension is reserved to the legislator alone and, except for his authentic interpretation, it is not enough to bring about an obligation of law.[49]

In regard to restrictive interpretation, Suarez applies the same principles which he had used in his discussion of the extension of law. It is enough to note here that he uses the term "restriction" when actually referring to broad or strict interpretation that remains within the proper natural or legal meaning of terms. He uses it likewise in connection with restriction which understands the terms of a law in a sense that is less than their proper meaning. For want of a better expression, this latter type of restriction may be referred to as restriction beyond the proper meaning of words.[50]

For Reiffenstuel, extension and restriction are divisions of interpretation considered in the proper sense. According to him, true interpretation seeks to determine the mind of the law and involves some departure from the words of the law.[51] Its main characteristic seems to be that it extends a law to cases not comprehended within its words. It supplies what is lacking to the words, and is called

[48] "Pure vero extensiva mens seu interpretatio dicitur illa per quam extenditur dispositio legis ad casum non comprehensum sub mente legislatoris propter similitudinem vel paritatem rationis."—*loc. cit.;* cf. White, *loc. cit.*

[49] Cf. White, *op. cit.,* pp. 14-16.

[50] *Op. cit.,* lib. VI, c. V, n. 1; cf. White, *ibid.,* p. 18.

[51] "Interpretatio autem proprie dicitur, quando a verbis legis receditur, et mens ejusdem ponderatur . . ."—*Jus Canonicum Universum,* lib. I, tit. II, n. 352.

by Reiffenstuel *interpretatio per modum suppletionis.* He concludes his description of it by stating that it is nothing more than a broadening of the scope of a law (*ampliatio*) based on the similarity or identity of the *ratio legis.*[52]

Reiffenstuel defines extensive interpretation, in general, as the broadening of the scope of the law to include what is not expressed in it.[53] He distinguishes between two types of extension in regard to law. If the interpretation goes beyond the words of the law and beyond the mind of the legislator, although not contrary to it, it is called extension in the proper sense.[54] If it proceeds beyond the words of the law but not beyond the mind of the legislator, it is extension only in the improper sense or comprehensive extension.[55]

Basically, the definition which Suarez and Reiffenstuel give for true extensive and comprehensive interpretation are identical. However, it would seem that Reiffenstuel's theory of extension differs somewhat from that of Suarez. As noted above, Suarez would not allow the extension of law because of a mere similarity of the *ratio legis.*[56] As White points out, Reiffenstuel does seem to admit such a possibility of extending the law, although his departure from Suarez on the point may be more verbal than real.[57]

Reiffenstuel contends that interpreters other than the authentic interpreter should attempt to discover the mind or intention of the

---

[52] "Per modum suppletionis fit interpretatio, quando declaratur obscuritas sensus legis, non spectando nudam litteram, et corticem verborum, sed verba simulque mentem ipsius, et sic declarando, quod lex ad hujusmodi casum sit extensa, vel non extensa. Et haec est proprie interpretatio: supplens, quod verbis legis deerat, sed non menti, nec aliud est, quam ampliatio quaedam, ex similitudine proveniens, vel identitate rationis . . ."—*ibid.,* n. 353.

[53] *Ibid.,* p. 370.

[54] "[Extensio proprie dicta] est illa, per quam cujuspiam legis decisio transfertur ad alium casum, vel personas, tam ultra verba legis, quam ultra mentem legislatoris, quamvis non contra mentem ipsius."—*ibid.,* n. 371.

[55] "Altera extensio, videlicet comprehensiva (quam etiam inclusivam et improprie dictam vocant) est illa, quae fit ultra verba legis, sed non ultra mentem legislatoris."—*loc. cit.*

[56] Cf. *supra,* p. 17.

[57] *Op. cit.,* p. 31.

legislator as expressed in the words which he uses. Where the meaning of the words of a law are doubtful, he would have the interpreter seek for the mind of the law in its matter and circumstances, but above all in the purpose of the law or the *ratio legis*.[58] Whereas Suarez had emphasized the role of the will of the legislator in interpretation, Reiffenstuel lays great stress on the purpose of the law as a norm of interpretation. With Suarez, he holds that where an *identical* purpose or reason is present for extending the law to other cases, the extension is to be considered as comprehensive. Unlike Suarez, however, he does not rule out completely the extension of a law because of a *similarity* of purpose. Reiffenstuel is not altogether clear on this point, but in effect, it does seem as though his emphasis on the *ratio legis* as a norm of interpretation leaves the way open for extension beyond the mind of the legislator.[59]

Reiffenstuel uses the term "restrictive" mainly in connection with strict interpretation. In one place where he defines restrictive interpretation as a narrowing of the meaning of the words of a law under the influence of equity, he employs examples which show that he is considering the notion of strict interpretation.[60] He does, however, mention restrictive interpretation that is extrinsic to, and not properly a part of, the law, in which case he is referring to the species of interpretation under discussion.[61] He gives a good description of the restrictive authentic interpretation of canon 17, when he uses the term *"derogatio"* to indicate an act whereby the legislator suppresses a part of a law and removes certain cases from its general provisions.[62]

Pre-Code authors after Suarez and Reiffenstuel differ as to their definition of extensive-restrictive and comprehensive interpretation. Whereas these two differed mainly on the question of the extension of law because of the similarity of the purpose or reason of the law, canonists after them begin to divide themselves, more or less, into two groups depending upon whether they emphasize

[58] *Op. cit.*, lib. I, c. II, nn. 384, 385.
[59] Cf. White, *op. cit.*, pp. 30, 31.
[60] *Op. cit.*, lib. I, c. II, n. 369.
[61] *Ibid.*, n. 376.
[62] *Ibid.*, n. 484.

the proper meaning of words or the mind of the legislator as the *terminus a quo* of extension and restriction. Both groups tend to avoid the use of the expression "pure extension."

Authors of the first group stress the proper meaning of the words of a law. For them, comprehensive interpretation becomes that which explains the sense of a law, doubtful according to the proper meaning of its words. They consider this to be interpretation in the proper sense.[63] Interpretation is extensive or restrictive in so far as it extends the words of a law beyond their proper meaning, or restricts them by narrowing the limits of their proper meaning.[64] According to Van Hove, this is the more common definition of extension and restriction.[65]

Authors of the second group emphasize the mind or intention of the legislator in defining extensive-restrictive and comprehensive interpretation. For them, interpretation that is comprehensive explains the meaning of a law according to the mind of the legislator. Extensive and restrictive interpretation extend or restrict the meaning of a law beyond the mind of the legislator. Michiels includes Palmieri, D'Annibale and Sebastianelli in this group.[66] It is not possible to place every author of this period into one or the other of these two categories. Some use the expression "comprehensive interpretation" when treating of interpretation that is merely declarative. Others speak of extension and restriction in regard to the interpretation of a doubtful law.[67] The division, however, is a useful one, for authors, in general, may be aggregated

---

[63] "Sola interpretatio comprehensiva sive declarativa, quae est explicatio legis dubiae et obscurae secundum proprium verborum sensum revera est interpretatio."—Wernz, *Ius Decretalium,* I, n. 128; cf. Schmalzgrueber (1663-1735), *Jus Ecclesiasticum Universum* (5 vols. in 12, Romae, 1843-1845), *Dissertatio Proemialis,* n. 373.

[64] "At per modestiam quandam etiam illa explicatio legis vocatur interpretatio, quae secundum proprietatem verborum data non est, sed aliquam mutationem legis habet admixtam, sive per extensionem ultra proprium sensum verborum ab initio in lege non contentum sive per restrictionem infra verborum sensum."—Wernz, *ibid.;* cf. Schmalzgrueber, *ibid.*

[65] *De Legibus,* n. 239.

[66] *Normae Generales,* I, 477, note 4.

[67] Cf. Van Hove, *loc. cit.*

to one or the other of the two groups. This division will be seen to be even more emphasized among authors after the Code.

Extensive and restrictive interpretation are not defined in the Code of Canon Law. The legislator does not even use any form of the term *"restrictio."* Canon 17, § 2 merely states that if the authentic interpretation of the law, given in the form of law, limits (*coarctet*) or extends the law, it does not have retroactive effect and must be promulgated. One may wonder why the Code employs the word *"coarctet"* instead of *"restringat"* when obviously referring to a form of restrictive interpretation. The reason is, that the legislator wished to be exact in the use of his terminology. According to canon 6, n. 2, canons of the Code which restate the old law without change must be interpreted upon the authority of the old law. In the decretalists, as noted already with regard to Suarez and Reiffenstuel, *interpretatio restrictiva* includes both restrictive and strict interpretation, two concepts which are not to be confused.[68] In order to avoid such confusion, the Code uses an altogether different term to convey the one idea of restrictive interpretation.[69] *Coarctare* means to restrict or limit, and as used by the legislator in canon 17, § 2 it means to limit the number of cases within the scope of the law. *Extendere* means to increase that number.[70] The Code considers both extension and restriction to be forms of interpretation, and, more particularly, of authentic interpretation. It avoids the use of the term *"comprehensiva"* and makes no mention of whether extension and restriction are to proceed beyond the words of a law or beyond the mind of the legislator.

Canonists after the Code continue to vary in their use of the terms under discussion in this division. A good number still speak of interpretation that is comprehensive when referring to extension. In general, those who hold the opinion that the point of departure for extensive interpretation is the mind of the legislator consider comprehensive interpretation to be that which goes beyond the proper meaning of the words but remains within the mind of the

[68] Cf. *supra*, pp. 17, 19.

[69] Cf. Schmidt, *The Principles of Authentic Interpretation*, pp. 203, 204.

[70] *Ibid.*, p. 220; cf. also Cicognani, *Canon Law*, p. 602.

legislator.[71] The authors, who maintain that the *terminus a quo* of extensive interpretation is the proper meaning of the words, often refer to interpretation that explains a doubtful or obscure law according to the proper meaning of its words as *interpretatio comprehensiva.*[72] Michiels holds that all interpretation is essentially comprehensive, in the sense that it merely makes known or declares what the legislator, in the beginning, intended should be included within the meaning of the words of a law, whether that meaning be the proper one or not.[73]

Since the promulgation of the Code, it would seem that the majority of canonists favor the opinion that extension and restriction should proceed from the words taken in their proper sense. Van Hove states that this is the position which he favors, and is the one more commonly accepted.[74]

Brys is of the opinion that, while philosophically there may be a distinction between extension and restriction *ultra vel infra verba legis* and extension and restriction *ultra vel infra mentem legislatoris,* juridically such a distinction is not to be admitted. He contends that, although in the final analysis the meaning of a law depends upon the will or intention of the legislator, the immediate concern of the interpreter should be the words which the lawgiver uses. Juridically, the external order of things is to be preferred and hence, the mind of the legislator is to be ascertained from the words by which he chooses to make known his intention. *De facto* there may be opposition between the two, but the presumption is that the legislative intent corresponds to the meaning of the words. Therefore, in the juridical order the comprehension

---

[71] Cf. Maroto, *Institutiones,* I, n. 236; Roelker, *Principles of Privilege According to the Code of Canon Law,* The Catholic University of America Canon Law Studies, n. 35 (Washington, D. C.: The Catholic University of America, 1926), p. 71 (hereafter cited *Principles of Privilege*) ; Vermeersch-Creusen, *Epitome,* I, n. 93.

[72] Cf. Brys, *Tractatus De Legibus,* p. 85; Cappello, *Summa Iuris Canonici,* 67.

[73] *Op. cit.,* I, pp. 476, 477.

[74] "Praeplacet terminologia quae interpretationem extensivam et restrictivam determinat relate ad sensum proprium verborum, non relate ad mentem et voluntatem legislatoris. Nam illa in iure canonico erat communius recepta et magis concordat cum definitione can. 17, § 2 . . ."—*op. cit.,* n. 241.

of a law, and its interpretation in general, are to be measured by the words of a law. Thus, in Brys' judgment, the point of departure for extension and restriction will be the words, and not the mind of the legislator.[75]

Schmidt reaches the same conclusion in discussing authentic interpretation that is extensive or restrictive. He cites Reiffenstuel to the effect that while words are to be understood according to their proper signification, the law must be made operative, if at all possible. As a result, the legal terminology must be taken, if necessary, in an improper sense. According to Schmidt, this is the principle of saving the law at all cost, a principle which is not to be admitted and is not provided for in the Code. He reasons that since canon 18 declares that laws are to be understood according to the proper sense of their words, no provision is made for the use of an improper meaning. He concludes by stating that "the restrictive or extensive interpretation envisioned by the Code proceeds upon the basis of the words taken in their proper meaning."[76]

One of the principal proponents of the opposing view is Michiels. His theory of interpretation rests on the contention that the proper meaning of words is not always the one intended by the legislator in phrasing a law. Although the legislator may not employ words in a purely arbitrary sense, it is conceivable that he will use them at times in a sense that is other than the proper one. It is necessary, then, for the interpreter to seek after the true meaning of the words. The true meaning is the one actually intended by the legislator, whether it be proper or improper. This theory of interpretation determines Michiels' notion of extension and restriction. In his opinion, interpretation that goes beyond the proper meaning of the words is not necessarily true extension. True extension goes beyond the true meaning of the words. Where the proper and the true meaning are the same, extension beyond the proper sense of the words will also be true extension. Where the two differ, extension beyond the proper, but within the true, meaning of the words is to be thought of as a form of interpreta-

---

[75] *Art. cit., Jus Pontificium,* XV (1935), 175-179.

[76] *Op. cit.,* pp. 212, 213.

tion in the strict sense. It is not true extension, but merely the explanation of what is contained in the law. According to Michiels' theory, then, the *terminus a quo* of restriction and extension is the mind of the legislator.[77]

White believes that interpretations given by the Code Commission tend to support Michiels' position. He, himself, defines extensive interpretation as that which "extends the provisions of the law to cases or persons which could in no hypothesis be conceived as included under any *real* sense of the verbal formula." Restrictive interpretation is that "which exempts certain persons or things from the provisions of a law under the real sense of whose verbal formula they indubitably come." By *real* he means the true sense of the words as intended by the legislator, and hence, his position is the same as that of Michiels.[78]

It will not be necessary, at this time, to attempt to resolve the controversy over the *terminus a quo* of extension and restriction in relation to law. The same question arises in a lesser degree in regard to rescripts. As will be seen later on, the proper meaning of the words constitutes the point of departure for extension and restriction in rescripts; and as a general rule such extension and restriction are not allowed. For the present it is enough to note that extension and restriction fall primarily within the province of authentic interpretation. Restrictive interpretation limits the number of persons or cases comprehended within the scope of a legal enactment. Extensive interpretation increases the number of persons or cases that are to be included within its scope.

C. Strict and Broad Interpretation

It is important to keep in mind the distinction between restrictive-extensive and strict-broad interpretation. The difference is not always clear in early canonical literature, and even a few modern authors seem to confuse the two types of interpretation. The principal difference between them is to be found in their object. Interpretation that is strict or broad is concerned primarily with the meaning of words, while restrictive and extensive interpretation

[77] *Op. cit.*, pp. 474-479.
[78] *Op. cit.*, pp. 7, 8.

depart from the meaning of words. In the brief historical survey that follows, it will be seen that by a gradual process of legal development the concepts of strict and broad interpretation became more precise, more liberated from the notions of restrictive and extensive interpretation. At present, however, there is controversy as to whether the proper meaning of the words, or the meaning intended by the legislator, constitutes the limits within which there is to be strict and broad interpretation. It is part of the same controversy noted in the previous subdivision concerning the point of departure for extension and restriction.

In his study of the historical development of the concept of strict interpretation, White contends that, along with the notion of broad interpretation, it had its origin in Roman Law, and that it evolved gradually as did the notion of interpretation itself.[79] In Canon Law, the most general expression of the two concepts is found in the axiom: *odia restringi et favores convenit ampliari.* The rule originated with the Roman Law glossator, Azo, and was used by other civilists to express the notions of strict and broad interpretation as found in Roman Law. It was adopted immediately as a norm for interpretation among canonists and later found its way into the *Liber Sextus* of Boniface VIII as Rule XV of the *"Regulae Juris."* Reference to the notion of strict interpretation, as well as to that which is broad, is found in Gratian in connection with the interpretation of penal law, prescription and privileges. In the collections which followed, there is frequent mention of certain types of laws and especially privileges, rescripts and dispensations that should be restricted or extended depending upon whether they are odious or favorable. In many instances it is evident that by restriction and extension is meant interpretation that is strict or broad, interpretation that is concerned primarily with words and whether they should be taken in a wide or narrow sense.[80]

Suarez was among the first to give a systematic presentation of the notions of strict and broad interpretation that clearly distinguishes them from restrictive and extensive interpretation. Al-

---

[79] *The Evolution of the Canonical Concept of Strict Interpretation of Law,* p. 6.

[80] *Ibid.,* pp. 46, 47.

though he refers to them in terms of restriction and extension, it is evident that he has the concepts of strict and broad interpretation clearly in mind. In his division of the various types of extension, he distinguishes between extension which stays within the proper meaning of terms and extension that goes beyond that meaning. He also makes a distinction between the natural and the legal proper meaning of terms, and considers interpretation that remains within the natural proper meaning, and interpretation which goes beyond the natural meaning but remains within the legal meaning of terms, as divisions of extension which stay within the proper meaning of terms.[81] Whereas Suarez permits extension or restriction which remains within the proper meaning of the words of the law depending upon whether the law is odious or favorable, he will not allow extension or restriction beyond the proper meaning, except where it is clearly evident that such extension or restriction is the will of the legislator, for example, where the reason or purpose of the law is identical.[82] From this it can be seen that he was aware of the distinction between strict-broad and restrictive-extensive interpretation. He shows that he was likewise fully cognizant of the notions of strict and broad interpretation, when he lays down the general rules that laws that are not odious are to be extended to include all that is contained within the natural meaning of the terms, and laws that are favorable are to be extended to the full measure of the proper meaning of the words, the legal as well as the natural.[83] A natural consequence of this is that laws which are odious are to be restricted to the narrowest sense that will still remain within the proper meaning of the words. Suarez does not actually say this in so many words, but it is deducible from what he has to say about extension and from the fact that he equivalates non-extension and restriction.[84]

In his discussion of the interpretation of rescripts, Pirhing (1606-1679) actually makes use of the term "strict" and "broad." In connection with the strict interpretation of rescripts *ad lites*

[81] *De Legibus*, lib. VI, c. II, n. 2.
[82] Cf. White, *op. cit.*, p. 13.
[83] *Op. cit.*, lib. VI, c. II, nn. 3-5.
[84] Cf. White, *op. cit.*, p. 12.

he calls attention to a rule that is particularly applicable. If a word can be taken in its proper sense, either in the generic and broad sense or in the specific and strict sense, then in doubt, if the intention of the one using the word cannot be ascertained, the word is to be understood strictly in odious matters and broadly in matters that are favorable or indifferent.[85] Since rescripts ad *lites* are to be considered as something odious, their terms are to be interpreted in the strict sense. He goes on to give examples of strict interpretation in such rescripts. Thus, according to Pirhing, in its strict connotation the word "cleric" does not include the bishop or religious; the term "people" does not comprise clerics.[86]

In Reiffenstuel, the concept of strict interpretation is clearly indicated. In most instances, he has in mind this type of interpretation when he speaks of *interpretatio restrictiva.* He defines it as a narrowing of the words of a law under the influence of equity. He mentions that the first part of the rule of law, *odia restringi et favores convenit ampliari,* has to do with this form of restrictive interpretation, and in like manner rescripts pertaining to the acquisition of benefices are to be restricted. For the same reason, he continues, the term "people" in an interdict does not include clerics. He concludes by stating that the same thing occurs in all matters that are said to be *"strictae interpretationis."*[87] Reiffenstuel refers to broad interpretation as *interpretatio ampla.* He states that favorable laws are to be understood in this way and adds, that in *materia favorabili* words are to be taken in their broad (*ampla*) meaning. The examples that he gives indicate that he has in mind the concept of broad interpretation. Thus, in doubt and where the matter is favorable, the word "people" includes clerics; the term "clerics" includes the bishop, canons and other ecclesiastical dignitaries; and the name of a given territory comprises exempt places as well as those not exempt.[88] For Reiffenstuel, then, strict and broad interpretation would seem to be that

[85] *Jus Canonicum in V Libros Decretalium* (4 vols., Dilingae, 1722), lib. I, tit. III, n. 23 (hereafter cited *Jus Canonicum*).

[86] *Loc. cit.*

[87] *Jus Canonicum Universum,* lib. I, tit. II, n. 369.

[88] *Ibid.*, n. 435.

which stays within the meaning of terms and is based now on a narrow and now on a wide understanding of words. It is not clear, however, whether the meaning of terms within which strict and broad interpretation fluctuate must necessarily be the proper meaning. In general, it may be said that Reiffenstuel uses the expression "restrictive interpretation" in opposition to broad interpretation (*interpretatio ampla*) rather than interpretation that is extensive. As was pointed out in the previous subdivision, however, he was aware of the notion of restrictive interpretation as opposed to that which is extensive.[89]

In the Code of Canon Law, legislation concerning strict and broad interpretation is to be found in canons 19, 50, 68 and 85. Canon 19 gives a list of laws that are to be strictly interpreted. Canon 50 gives an enumeration of the rescripts that are to receive a strict interpretation and adds that all others are to be broadly interpreted. Canons 68 and 85 set forth similar legislation for privileges and dispensations. No explicit mention is made in these canons of odious and favorable matters. Pre-Code authors went to great lengths in their efforts to distinguish between *odia* and *favorabilia* in order to find out when an interpretation should be strict and when it should be broad. The legislator in the Code purposely avoids such an attempt, and, instead, gives a taxative enumeration of the laws, rescripts, etc., that are subject to strict interpretation. In regard to the notions of strict and broad interpretation, the Code makes no attempt to define them; nor is this necessary, since the concepts are clear enough as set forth in approved pre-Code authors. The legislator does not state in so many words that strict and broad interpretation must necessarily fall within the proper meaning of words, although canon 19 taken in conjunction with canon 18, and canon 50 taken in conjunction with canon 49 seem to imply that this is so. As will be seen in the discussion to follow immediately, the majority of modern canonists are of this opinion. It is sufficient to note here, that the Code speaks of strict and broad interpretation only in connection with doubt, and as norms of interpretation considers them within the scope of doctrinal interpretation.

[89] Cf. *supra*, p. 19.

Among the majority of commentators on the Code, interpretation is strict or broad depending upon whether the proper meaning of words is taken in a narrow or wide sense. The same definition is repeated over and over again in a number of authors.[90] Brems conveys the same idea in different words when he defines strict interpretation as that which comprehends what *must* be understood within the proper meaning of the terms of a law, and broad interpretation as that which includes what *may* be understood within these terms.[91] Strict interpretation limits the proper meaning of words to the narrowest confines that will still permit them to have some effect. Broad interpretation extends them as much as possible. Both always remain within the proper meaning of the words, according to what would seem to be the more common opinion.[92] According to the authors who favor this opinion, this is the chief characteristic which distinguishes them from restrictive and extensive interpretation, which depart from the proper signification of terms. In addition, strict and broad interpretation fall primarily within the province of doctrinal interpretation, while interpretation that is restrictive and extensive lies within the exclusive competence of the authentic interpreter.[93]

Toso seems to equivalate strict and broad interpretation with that which is non-extensive and extensive. In treating of the question of extension or non-extension because of the *finis legis* or the mind of the legislator, he remarks that strict interpretation is according to the proper meaning of the words, while broad interpretation goes beyond that meaning.[94]

For Michiels, interpretation is strict or broad depending upon

---

[90] "Stricta interpretatio intellegit verba sensu proprio sed magis coarctato, lata sensu proprio sed magis extenso . . ."—Van Hove, *De Legibus,* n. 242; cf. also Beste, *Introductio in Codicem,* p. 77; Brys, *Tractatus De Legibus,* p. 85; Cappello, *Summa Iuris Canonici,* p. 67.

[91] "De Interpretatione Authentica Codicis J. C. Per Pont. Commissionem," *Jus Pontificium,* XV (1935), 180.

[92] In addition to the authors cited above cf. Coronata, *Institutiones,* I, n. 25; Schmidt, *The Principles of Authentic Interpretation,* pp. 218, 219; Vermeersch-Creusen, *Epitome,* I, n. 93.

[93] Cf. Schmidt, *loc. cit.*

[94] *Commentaria Minora ad Codicem Iuris Canonici* (5 vols., Taurini-Romae, 1921-1927), I, 61 (hereafter cited *Commentaria Minora*).

whether the meaning of words as intended by their author is taken in a narrow or wide sense. He will not go along with the more common opinion that this type of interpretation operates within the confines of the proper signification of terms. He believes that their limits are determined by the true meaning of the words, and that, while the proper sense will ordinarily be the one intended by the author, and hence the true sense, this is not always the case. He feels that there are times when the strict meaning will have to be something less than the proper one, and in like manner there will be occasions when an improper meaning of words will have to be considered as the broad or wide understanding of terms. In short, the intention of the one using the words will often indicate that they are to be understood in such a way that their strict or broad interpretation will have to depart from the proper meaning.[95]

White is among those who favor the same position held by Michiels. He points out that the intention of the legislator, as manifested in the words that he uses, must conform in some way to the meaning of those words as accepted in common speech or in juridical language. In brief, the legislator may not use words in such a way that they depend upon his arbitrary will. White feels, however, that there are times when words might be employed in a way that would make it difficult to say that the legislator is using them according to their proper signification. He concedes that it would be an unreasonable use of words to allow the legislator to depart far from their proper meaning, but he believes that one should not insist on a too narrow notion of the proper meaning, nor confine the legislator to the latest dictionary definitions. Therefore, he would allow the legislator to go beyond the proper meaning of words to what is considered a reasonable use of terms. White calls this the reasonably real meaning of the words. According to him, words may be taken in a narrow or a broad sense, and yet both of these meanings will be the proper or at least the reasonably real meaning. Hence, he defines strict interpretation as a restriction of law by taking the words in the narrowest sense that remains within their reasonably real meaning, and broad

---

[95] Cf. *Normae Generales,* I, 481, note 1.

interpretation as an extension of law by taking the words in the broadest sense compatible with a real meaning of the words.[96]

It is somewhat difficult to see how there can be strict or broad interpretation within the true meaning of words as Michiels contends, or within the real sense as White would have it. The meaning intended by the author must necessarily be one, either strict or broad, since the legislator can not at the same time intend that his words be taken in a narrow or a wide sense. Michiels himself admits this, but adds that when he affirms that the meaning intended by the legislator can be understood at times in a strict or broad sense, he has in mind the meaning arrived at by the application of the rules in canon 18. He believes that the application of these rules will sometimes reveal that the meaning intended by the legislator is narrower than the proper meaning of the words, and at other times will disclose that his intended meaning is actually wider or more extensive than the proper signification. Michiels considers the former to be strict interpretation and the latter to be broad interpretation, and thus, the two are said to be within the meaning of the words as intended by the legislator. Where doubt persists as to which meaning is intended, then canon 19 must be followed.[97]

---

[96] *Op. cit.*, p. 8.

[97] *Op. cit.*, I, pp. 481, 482.

CHAPTER II

The Notion and Divisions of Rescripts

INTRODUCTION

The previous chapter was devoted to a survey of the notion and divisions of interpretation. The present chapter will be concerned with a similar survey of the notion and divisions of rescripts. Its principal purpose will be to give a clear idea of what a rescript is and to discuss in some detail those divisions of rescripts which are important in regard to their interpretation. Frequent reference will be made to pre-Code canonists in explaining the notion and divisions of rescripts. Together with the concept of a rescript, they evolved the various divisions that are found in nearly all commentaries on the Code. In addition, they made several distinctions which, while not repeated as such by modern authors, are of some importance, for they recur often in pre-Code literature and will be referred to in later chapters.

ARTICLE I. THE NOTION OF A RESCRIPT

In general, a rescript is a written reply in answer to a request. Taken in its widest sense, the term "rescript" could be applied to every written response that is given, even by a private individual, in answer to another's petition.[1] In its legal acceptation, however, a rescript is an answer given in writing by someone in authority. According to pre-Code jurisprudence, it was considered to be a written reply given by one in highest authority (*a Principe*), such as the Pope in ecclesiastical affairs or the Emperor in secular matters.[2] Replies issued in writing by ecclesiastical superiors inferior to the Roman Pontiff were simply called letters or given some other designation.[3] Since the promulgation of the Code, how-

[1] Schmalzgrueber, *Jus Ecclesiasticum Universum,* lib. I, tit. III, n. 1.

[2] Pirhing, *Jus Canonicum,* lib. I, tit. III, n. 1.

[3] "Porro litterae inferiorum v.g. episcoporum, vix dicuntur rescripta, sed magis usitate appellantur litterae, v.g. absolutionis, excommunicationis et hujusmodi . . ."—Reiffenstuel, *Jus Canonicum Universum,* lib. I, tit. III, n. 3.

ever, rescripts in the ecclesiastical forum are no longer considered to be the exclusive prerogative of the Pope. The Code itself speaks of rescripts of the Apostolic See as well as those of other Ordinaries.[4]

A rescript is first of all a reply. A reply, or answer, presupposes a question of some sort. In like manner a rescript presupposes a petition or request. In Canon Law a rescript is an answer given by an ecclesiastical superior to someone's inquiry. Examples of this are found in the decretal letters which form the bulk of the *Corpus Iuris Canonici*. The majority of these letters are actually rescripts, or replies, given in answer to a petition. This is often evident from the very first word of a letter which indicates that an inquiry of some sort has preceded.[5] This is the main feature that distinguishes a rescript from a decree. The former is a direct answer to some previous inquiry, while the latter is not an answer to a specific inquiry, but rather a letter sent entirely on the initiative of the Holy See.[6] Decrees are usually Acts of the Roman Congregations and are issued principally in the administrative order. They are independent of any earlier requests or inquiries that may have been received about the matter with which they are concerned.

At times a rescript may be granted *motu proprio*. When such a phrase is inserted in a reply, it does not follow that the rescript was not issued in answer to some petition. The phrase "*motu proprio*" merely signifies that the rescript has been granted out of the free choice and liberality of its author and not only because of the reasons set forth in the petition. A rescript is always granted at the instance (*ad instantiam*) of someone. On occasion, the Holy Father may wish to show that he is granting the favor, not because of the motives alleged in the request, but on his own initiative. In such a case, he inserts the phrase "*motu proprio.*"

---

[4] Cf. cans. 36, § 1, 43, 44, 61.

[5] "Unde in diversis capitulis juris canonici, utpote quod secundum magnam sui partem ex decretalibus epistolis, seu rescriptis summorum Pontificum compilatum fuit, passim occurrunt hujusmodi initia: 'Consuluisti, consuluit, insinuante, insinuatum est, significasti' et hujusmodi."—Reiffenstuel, *op. cit.*, lib. I, tit. III, n. 2.

[6] Cf. O'Neill, *Papal Rescripts of Favor*, p. 4.

When the phrase is absent, it indicates that the favor is being granted on account of the motives proposed in the petition. Such a rescript is said to be given *ad instantiam,* or *ad preces.*[7]

The petition which occasions a rescript may contain different types of requests or inquiries. The object of the petition may be to seek information, advice or guidance, or to obtain some favor, dispensation or privilege. So, too, a rescript may have as its object a variety of matters. This can be seen in the definition of a rescript as given by the early as well as the late pre-Code authors.[8] A rescript may be concerned with a judicial matter, some doubt of law, a disciplinary problem or the concession of a favor. Many of the rescripts in the *Corpus Iuris Canonici* are concerned with the interpretation of ecclesiastical discipline and doctrine, as well as questions of law. Rescripts delegating judges and regulating the formalities in judicial processes are also to be found in great numbers in the various collections. Included, too, are rescripts granting benefices, dispensations, privileges, indulgences, honors, degrees and various other favors and permissions. These are but examples of the wide range of topics that may form the subject matter of a rescript. At present, dispensations, especially matrimonial dispensations, are the most numerous of all the different kinds of rescripts that are granted by the Holy See, as well as other Ordinaries.[9]

A rescript is a written reply. Not any and every answer that is given in reply to a petition is to be considered as a rescript. It is necessary that the reply be made in writing. In Roman Law, rescripts known as *Epistolae* were brief and informal answers written on a document separate from the inquiry. *Subscriptiones* or *Adnotationes* were replies written on the side or the bottom of the petition itself.[10] The very name "rescript" indicates that a

---

[7] Cicognani, *Canon Law,* p. 698; O'Neill, *loc. cit.*

[8] "[Rescriptum] est illud, quod ab Apostolico, i.e., a Papa, seu a Principe rescribitur ad consultationem, relationem, seu intimationem alterius, vel alicui indulgendo."—Panormitanus (+ 1453), *Commentaria in Quinque Libros Decretalium* (5 vols. in 7, Venetiis, 1588), lib. I, tit. III, in rubricam, n. 1 (hereafter cited *Commentaria*). The same definition is more or less repeated by later commentators. Cf. Reiffenstuel, *op. cit.,* lib. I, tit. III, n. 2.

[9] Cf. O'Neill, *op. cit.,* p. 17.

[10] O'Neill, *op. cit.,* p. 6.

written document is required, and writing has always been considered essential to the nature of a rescript. Thus, a rescript is distinguished from an answer that is given by word of mouth, the so-called *Oraculum Vivae Vocis,* which is an oral reply of the Pope or one of the Dicasteries of the Roman Curia. Although the reply may be put in writing after it is given, this is only for the sake of proof and does not make a rescript of it.

A rescript may be looked upon as the legal instrument by means of which an ecclesiastical superior (the Apostolic See or a subordinate Ordinary) makes known his mind or intention relative to a particular request. It is the written document which conveys to the petitioner the information, counsel, delegation, permission, etc., that he has sought. The chief function of a rescript is to communicate a reply. The nature of the reply will be determined to a great extent by the tenor of the petition. The petition itself may be oral, but a request in writing is usual and to be expected. The answer, of course, must be in writing to constitute a rescript.

In the ecclesiastical forum, then, a rescript may be defined as a reply given in writing by the Apostolic See or a subordinate Ordinary in answer to a petition that may request a favor, ask for information, seek specific instructions and the like.

ARTICLE II. THE DIVISIONS OF RESCRIPTS

Various divisions of rescripts can be made depending upon the author, the manner in which a rescript is issued, its relation to the subject matter or the common law and so forth. It will not be necessary to enter into a discussion of all the divisions of rescripts that have been made by authors both before and after the Code. Certain divisions, however, have special importance in regard to the interpretation of rescripts. Particular attention will be paid to these.

Section 1. Rescripts in Relation to the Common Law

With respect to the common law, rescripts are according to the law (*secundum*), outside the law (*praeter*) or contrary to the law (*contra legem*). In general, rescripts are according to the law when they promote its observance. They are outside the law when they decide some point not defined by the law. They are contrary to the law when they grant something that is against, or in opposition to, the law.[11] Each one of these divisions can be considered separately in some detail.

A rescript according to the law (*secundum ius*) is often referred to in pre-Code jurisprudence as a rescript in the strict sense.[12] Pirhing describes it as a rescript which is given according to the common law or to further the observance of the law, as when a superior (*Princeps*) commits to someone the power to judge and decide some controversy between parties, gives an answer concerning doubts of law or decides, in a particular matter, what should be done according to the prescriptions of law. He, too, refers to such a written reply as a rescript in the strict sense.[13] The idea he wishes to convey is that, strictly speaking, a rescript should not run counter to the law. Its main purpose is to protect the law, insure its observance and to point out, if necessary in a given situation, what the law demands. Thus, a request might be received asking for the settlement of a controversy. In answer, a judge could be appointed whose duty it is to see that the controversy is settled according to the law. In another instance, a petition might contain an inquiry concerning some doubt of law. A rescript will be issued giving the correct interpretation or understanding of the law. Finally, the author of a petition might know the law, but at the same time he may have uncertainties as to its application in a particular case. Therefore, he will petition higher authorities for information and guidance. The rescript will contain instructions on how to resolve the case in accord with the requirements of the law.

All of the rescripts mentioned as examples by Pirhing have one thing in common. They do not deviate from the law. Considered in relation to the law, all of them are seen to be in conformity with the law. They are legal instruments issued to further or pro-

---

[11] Cicognani, *op. cit.*, p. 698.

[12] "Sed rescriptum stricte et in specie sumptum, dicitur illud, quod emanat ad observantiam iuris communis."—Rubrica ad *de rescriptis,* I, 3 in VI; cf. also Panormitanus, *Commentaria,* lib. I, tit. III, in Rubricam, n. 2; Schmalzgrueber, *op. cit.,* lib. I, tit. III, n. 1.

[13] *Jus Canonicum,* lib. I, tit. III, n. 2.

mote the observance of the law. Whether they are called rescripts in the strict sense or rescripts *secundum ius,* they are a means employed to expedite matters according to the prescriptions of the law.

In the *Corpus Iuris Canonici* it is not unusual to find the term "rescript" used without any qualification to denote a rescript in the strict sense or a rescript *secundum ius.* Thus, a gloss to the *Liber Sextus* mentions that if a rescript grants something contrary to the law, then it is not to be called a rescript but a privilege.[14] The same use of the term is evident in many of the early decretalists.[15]

Pre-Code authors very often referred to rescripts contrary to the law and rescripts outside the law simply as privileges, dispensations or *beneficia Principis.* Such rescripts were often called rescripts in the broad sense to distinguish them from rescripts in the strict sense (rescripts in conformity with the law). Many of the authors gave to the term "rescript" a narrow and a wide meaning. As pointed out already, the narrow meaning of the term denoted but one type of rescript, the rescript *secundum ius.*[16] The wide meaning of the term included not only rescripts in the strict sense, but all other types of rescripts as well. The authors mention in particular privileges, dispensations and *beneficia* (favors), but from the definitions which they give and the distinctions which they make concerning these terms, it is clear that they have in mind rescripts contrary to the law and rescripts outside the law.[17]

Panormitanus states that the term "rescript" can be taken in the general or broad sense, and then it includes a privilege, *beneficium Principis,* and rescripts which further the observance of the law (*quae emanant ad iuris observantiam*). A privilege he describes

---

[14] *Glossa ordinaria* ad c. 2, *de constitutionibus,* I, 2, s.v. *Noscatur.*

[15] Cf. Innocent IV (1243-1254), *In V Libros Decretalium Commentaria* (Venetiis, 1570), lib. I, tit. III, c. 18, n. 2 (hereafter cited *Commentaria*); Panormitanus, *Commentaria,* lib. I, tit. III, c. 18, n. 1.

[16] Cf. *supra,* p. 36.

[17] Cf. Rubrica ad *de rescriptis,* I, 3 in VI; Panormitanus, *Commentaria,* lib. I, tit. III, in Rubricam, n. 2; Reiffenstuel, *Jus Canonicum Universum,* lib. I, tit. III, nn. 15-18; Schmalzgrueber, *Jus Ecclesiasticum Universum,* lib. I, tit. III, n. 1.

as a rescript contrary to the law. A *beneficium* is a favor granted outside the law.[18]

According to Pirhing, the term "rescript" can be used in the broad sense for every privilege and *beneficium Principis* that is obtained in writing. He goes on to add that a privilege is granted by a superior *"ad aliquid agendum, vel non agendum contra jus commune."* He includes dispensations also within this definition. His notion of *beneficium* is the same as that given by Panormitanus.[19]

In listing the various types of rescripts in the broad sense, Reiffenstuel mentions that privileges, dispensations, etc., as well as rescripts in the strict sense can be termed rescripts inasmuch as they are written replies in answer to a petition.[20] In general, he classifies a privilege as a rescript granted contrary to the law and a *beneficium* in the strict sense as a rescript granting a favor outside the law. He is careful to mention, however, that a privilege can also be outside the law, and that a *beneficium* in the broad sense could include any favor even though it be contrary to the law or outside of it.[21]

In effect, the division which considers rescripts in the broad sense is no different from that which considers them on the basis of whether they are in conformity with the law, contrary to it, or outside of it. This is noted by Pirhing in the introduction to his study of rescripts.[22] In treating of the division, the authors mention in particular rescripts which further the observance of the law, privileges and dispensations which are contrary to the law and *beneficia* which are outside of the law. What they actually do, then, is to distinguish various types of rescripts depending upon their relation to the law. However, instead of merely stating that

---

[18] *Loc. cit.*

[19] *Jus Canonicum,* lib. I, tit. III, n. 2.

[20] "Nam quodlibet horum consistit in certis literis, sive epistolis quibus Pontifex rescribit, atque respondet sibi supplicantibus, concedendo ipsis gratiam, beneficium, vel aliquid ordinando pertinens ad juris observantiam." —*op. cit.*, lib. I, tit. III, n. 15.

[21] *Ibid.*, nn. 17, 18.

[22] "Sumitur autem hoc loco rescriptum late ac generaliter, prout omne privilegium et beneficium Principis ideoque litteras, sive secundum jus, sive contra, vel praeter jus, concessas complectitur."—*op. cit.,* lib. I, tit. III, n. 2.

rescripts may be *secumdum, contra* or *praeter ius,* they make mention of the different kinds of rescripts and then point out which ones are contrary to the law and which ones are outside of the law and so forth. Rescripts in the strict sense are always according to the law. Dispensations are always contrary to it. Privileges in general are contrary to the law but may be outside of it. *Beneficia* in the strict sense are outside of the law, but the term itself has a wider meaning that includes any rescript that proves favorable to the recipient.[23]

Canonical authors since the Code seldom make mention of rescripts in the strict and broad sense as such. They prefer to use the term "rescript" in its broad meaning to include every type of rescript, whether it be a privilege, a dispensation, a simple favor or a rescript that is in conformity with the law. In considering the relation of rescripts to the common law, they designate them simply as rescripts *secundum, contra,* or *praeter legem.* This division of rescripts is not a new one, for it is found among the early pre-Code canonists[24] and was in use even before authors began to distinguish between rescripts in the strict and broad sense. Reiffenstuel incorporates both divisions in his commentary on the title *"De Rescriptis."*[25]

In the final analysis, all written responses of the Apostolic See and subordinate Ordinaries that tend to further the observance of

---

[23] Cf Reiffenstuel, *op. cit.*, lib. I, tit. III, nn. 15-19. It may be noted here that the term *"beneficium"* is often used by pre-Code authors when discussing rescripts. In general it is defined as a "benevola actio gaudium tribuens capienti." In its strict acceptation, the term is reserved for a favor (*liberalitas quaedam*) which is prejudicial to no one and is outside the law. Taken in its wide sense, the term is applied to a privilege that is contrary to the law and also to a rescript that is *secundum jus.* The latter is called a *beneficium* in the very wide sense that the superior who issues the rescript is not forced to do so, and is therefore bestowing a favor of a sort on the petitioner.—Panormitanus, *Commentaria,* lib. V, tit. XL, c. 16, n. 7; cf. also Reiffenstuel, *op. cit.,* lib. I, tit. II, n. 445.

[24] St. Raymond of Peñafort (1180-1275), *Opera Omnia* (Curante Rmo. Dre. Josepho Reus et Serra, Barchinonae, 1945-   ), I (*Summa Iuris*), Pars Prima, VII (*De Rescriptis Et Eorum Interpretationibus*); Hostiensis (+ 1271), *Summa Aurea* (Venetiis, 1570), lib. I, tit. III, n. 9.

[25] Cf. nn. 15-22.

the law are to be considered as rescripts according to the law. The designation *"secundum ius"* is used to distinguish this type of rescript from those that are in opposition to the law or that decide some point not defined by the law. Some rescripts are designed principally to expedite matters according to the requirements of law. They contain nothing that is not already stated in the law. Therefore, they are said to be *secundum ius* or in keeping with the law.[26]

As the name implies, rescripts *contra legem* are those that are contrary to the prescriptions of law. They contain answers that make exception to the law. The majority of these rescripts will be either privileges *contra legem* or dispensations. Rescripts outside or beyond the law (*praeter legem*) are those that grant favors or confer powers which neither come under any provision of law nor are opposed to any of its enactments, for example, indulgences, faculties and certain privileges.[27]

The interpretation which is to be given to a rescript in a particular case may depend upon whether the rescript is in conformity with the law, contrary to the law or outside the law. Therefore, the division which considers rescripts and their relation to the common law is a useful one in regard to the interpretation of rescripts, and will be referred to again in several of the chapters that follow.

Section 2. Rescripts in Relation to Their Subject Matter

Considered from the point of view of their subject matter, rescripts are usually divided into rescripts of justice (*iustitiae*) and rescripts of favor (*gratiae*). The former are also referred to as rescripts *ad lites* (pertaining to legal suits). To this division is sometimes added a third category known as mixed rescripts

---

[26] According to Michiels, rescripts *secundum ius* "conceduntur ad urgendam vel confirmandam ipsius juris observantiam, dando facultatem aut licentiam ad normam juris impetrandam ut quid legitime fiat, puta rescriptum quo datur legitimi Superioris beneplacitum ad alienationem certorum bonorum ecclesiasticorum requisitum, vel rescriptum quo designatur judex specialis ad judicamdum de causa determinata";—*Normae Generales,* II, 286.

[27] Cf. O'Neill, *op. cit.*, pp. 2, 3.

(*rescripta mixta*). This is the most important as well as the most ancient of all the different divisions of rescripts.[28]

A. Rescripts of Justice

Rescripts of justice have their origin in Roman Law. In their original form they were written replies which sought to explain the law and thereby to insure the administration of justice in the various parts of the Empire. They were issued by the Emperor himself, and in the course of time they came to be known as rescripts of justice. Beginning with the reign of the Emperor Hadrian (117-130), letters of this sort were issued in increasing numbers to judges as well as to private individuals who were involved in litigation of some kind. Judges frequently found themselves in a position where they had to petition the Emperor for advice in the solution of difficult court cases. If the Emperor deemed it necessary to intervene in the case, he sent back a written reply, or rescript. Contained in the rescript would be the decision on the case or the principle upon which the judge was to base his final decision. Under certain circumstances, the individuals involved in the litigation were also allowed to petition the Emperor for a ruling in their case. If the Emperor decided to answer the inquiry of the individual instead of allowing the case to go through the ordinary court procedure, he sent his decision directly to the petitioner, who then had the option of using the rescript or disregarding it as he saw fit. The recipient could exercise his right to use the rescript even after a long lapse of time, and in the event that he died before availing himself of its benefit, his heirs still retained the option. Once a rescript was received, however, the judge in the case could no longer decide the matter according to his own convictions, but was obligated to render a decision according to the ruling or the principle contained in the reply, even though the rescript be addressed to one of the litigants rather than to himself.[29]

Rescripts similar to the Roman rescripts of justice are also found in the Canonical sources. Just as the Roman Emperors were

---

[28] O'Neill, *op. cit.*, p. 2.

[29] O'Neill, *op. cit.*, pp. 7, 9, 10; cf. also Buckland, *A Textbook of Roman Law* (2. ed., Cambridge: University Press, 1932), pp. 665, 666.

often requested to render a decision or give advice in the solution of difficult legal suits, so too, the Roman Pontiffs were often petitioned for help and instructions in the settlement of judicial disputes. Many of their replies are found among the decretal letters included in the *Corpus Iuris Canonici.*[30] They are designated by canonical authors as rescripts of justice, or rescripts *ad lites.* In general, they contain instructions and regulations governing the conduct of legal suits and the administration of justice. In some of the rescripts the Popes, as the Roman Emperors before them had done, give the decision which is to be applied to the case. In many instances, however, the decision is left up to the local tribunal, and the written replies contain, instead, the appointment of a judge to handle the matter along with instructions to be followed in conducting the process, as well as the explanation of doubtful points of law and the like.[31]

In general, then, rescripts of justice are those which contain provisions relating to legal suits and the administration of justice. They are called rescripts of justice because they deal with matters connected with courts of justice, e.g., the delegations of judges, the formalities to be observed in a trial and so forth. Since court trials involve litigation, this type of written reply is also referred to as a rescript *ad litem.*

A distinction is usually made between rescripts of justice and rescripts of favor. The distinction is not based on the fact that one type of rescript contains a favor and the other does not. A favor can be bestowed in a rescript of justice as well as in a rescript of favor. The main difference between the two is to be found in their subject matter. Rescripts of justice are concerned primarily with judicial matters and legal suits. As will be seen in the discussion to follow, rescripts of favor contain dispensations, priv-

---

[30] "Et talia rescripta passim in toto corpore juris canonici occurrunt."—Reiffenstuel, *op. cit.,* lib. I, tit. III, n. 28.

[31] "Rescripta justitiae seu ad lites sunt illa, quae per principem expediuntur ad delegationem, seu decisionem causarum judicialium; ut si Papa causae ad se devolutae judicem delegatum constituat, vel quando de jure partium obscuro consultus interpretatur illud, et quid judex in judicando sequi debet, declarat."—Reiffenstuel, *loc. cit.*

ileges and other favors in no way connected with judicial matters and litigation.[32]

Rescripts of justice may also contain favors, or *gratiae*. As Santi points out, a rescript always implies a concession or favor on the part of the superior who issues it.[33] Commenting on a particular decretal letter containing a rescript of justice, Panormitanus refers to the fact that, in issuing the rescript, the Pope was considered to have granted a favor, even though he made no concession that was contrary to the law. The reason for this, he adds, is that the petitioner who requested the particular rescript *ad lites* could have settled the matter with his own Ordinary, instead of petitioning Rome for a solution to his case.[34] The implication, of course, is that the Supreme Pontiff, in answering the petition, was doing the recipient of the rescript a favor. The same is true of any rescript of justice, for one or both of the parties involved in a case will always benefit by it.[35]

For the most part, rescripts of justice will be *secundum ius*. This is understandable in view of their object, which is to protect the rights of individuals and moral persons. Whether a rescript of justice is one in which a case is decided, a judge delegated to try it or an obscure right explained, its purpose will be to see that justice is done, and that the rights of the parties involved in a dispute are safeguarded. Most of these rights will be determined to a large extent by law. Therefore, the superior who issues the rescript will be anxious to see to it that the matter under dispute is settled according to the prescriptions of the law. The rescript, then, will be *secundum ius*. In some instances, disputes will arise that are not covered by the law. When this happens, rescripts may be issued containing provisions for settling the dispute. The matter

---

[32] In discussing the difference between rescripts of justice and rescripts of favor, Santi states: "Haec distinctio non procedit ex eo quod secundi generis tantum rescripta contineant favorem; rescriptum enim semper exhibet liberalitatem et gratiam Principis. Sed distinctio procedit ex diversitate objecti seu materiae";—*Praelectiones Juris Canonici* (2. ed., 5 vols. in 2, Ratisbonae, Neo Eboraci et Cincinnatii, 1892), lib. I, tit. III, n. 3 (hereafter cited *Praelectiones*).

[33] *Loc. cit.*

[34] *Commentaria,* lib. I, tit. III, c. 28, n. 1.

[35] Cf. Michiels, *op. cit.,* II, 287.

will be handled, then, according to directives that are outside the law, and the rescript itself will be *praeter ius*.

B. Rescripts of Favor

Rescripts of favor also have their origin in Roman Law. In addition to inquiries about the law and requests for decisions and advice in judicial matters, letters were also sent to the Emperors in which the petitioner sought an exception to the law or some sort of favor, such as a dispensation or privilege. The answers of the Emperors to these petitions for favors were commonly called *Personales Constitutiones*. In general, they granted to the individual a certain right to a particular object, some power or permission to which he had no previous claim, e.g., a dispensation, pecuniary assistance or legitimation of children.[36] The *Personales Constitutiones* were never called rescripts of favor as such, and authors who contend that rescripts in Roman Law were always in accordance with the law are unwilling to classify them even as rescripts. Nevertheless, among modern authors there are many who do not hesitate to refer to them as rescripts of favor.[37]

In Canon Law, rescripts of favor (*gratiae*) are written replies which contain dispensations, privileges, indulgences and the like that are granted as a result of the free choice and generosity of their author,[38] and which are connected in no way with judicial contentions.[39] They are called rescripts of favor because they bestow benefits and favors (*gratiae*) to which the recipient has no legal title. They are distinguished from rescripts of justice by reason of the fact that they are concerned primarily with granting a favor and not with litigation, the protection of rights, and the administration of justice. Instead of explaining the law, they usually make exceptions to it, and as a result they are often contrary to the law. They are outside the law when they grant favors, e.g., indulgences, honors, permissions, that are neither contrary to the law nor covered by any provision of the law.

---

[36] O'Neill, *op. cit.*, pp. 7-9; cf. also Van Hove, *De Rescriptis*, p. 8.

[37] O'Neill, *loc. cit.*

[38] Pirhing, *op. cit.*, lib. I, tit. III, n. 4.

[39] Santi, *Praelectiones*, lib. I, tit. III, n. 3; Cicognani, *Canon Law*, p. 697.

C. Mixed Rescripts

In treating of rescripts in relation to their subject matter, canonists have introduced a third category of rescripts called mixed rescripts, which combine in one written reply elements which are proper to rescripts of justice and rescripts of favor. A mixed rescript is one that contains, at the same time, provisions pertaining to legal suits or the administration of justice, and favors which are not connected in any way with judicial affairs. A rescript need not be limited in its subject matter. As in the example given by Reiffenstuel, a rescript may confer a benefice, and at the same time contain provisions for the appointment of someone whose duty it will be to make sure that the rights of the beneficiary are protected.[40] Such a rescript is referred to as a *rescriptum mixtum.*

[40] *Op. cit.*, lib. I, tit. III, n. 31.

PART II

The General Norms for the Interpretation of Rescripts

INTRODUCTION

The Code of Canon Law contains two principal canons which determine the norms to be followed in the interpretation of rescripts. They are canon 49 and canon 50. According to canon 49: *Rescripta intelligenda sunt secundum propriam verborum significationem et communem loquendi usum, nec debent ad casus alios praeter expressos extendi.* Canon 50 states: *In dubio, rescripta quae ad lites referuntur, vel iura aliis quaesita laedunt, vel adversantur legi in commodum privatorum, vel denique impetrata fuerunt ad beneficii ecclesiastici assecutionem, strictam interpretationem recipiunt; cetera omnia latam.*

In addition to these two canons, there are three others in the Code which regulate the interpretation of special types of rescripts. They are canons 67, 68 and 85. The first two are concerned with the interpretation of privileges. According to canon 67: *Privilegium ex ipsius tenore aestimandum est, nec licet illud extendere aut restringere.* Canon 68 reads: *In dubio privilegia interpretanda sunt ad normam can. 50; sed ea semper adhibenda interpretatio, ut privilegio aucti aliquam ex indulgentia concedentis videantur gratiam consecuti.* Canon 85 governs the interpretation of dispensations. It states: *Strictae subest interpretationi non solum dispensatio ad normam can. 50, sed ipsamet facultas dispensandi ad certum casum concessa.*

In the very last canon of the title on rescripts in the Code (can. 62), the legislator lays down the rule that if a rescript contains not a simple favor, but a privilege or a dispensation, then the prescriptions of the canons pertaining to privileges and dispensations are also to be followed, as well as those in canons 49 and 50. Therefore, if a rescript contains a privilege, canons 67 and 68 are applicable. Except for certain modifications, however, the legislation contained in these two canons is the same as that found in canons 49 and 50. When a dispensation or the faculty to dispense in a particular case is granted in a rescript, canon 85 directs that the prescriptions of canon 50 are to be followed.

The rules contained in the afore-mentioned canons can be divided into two categories. The rules prescribed in canons 49 and 67 are general norms for the interpretation of rescripts, while those indicated in canons 50 and 68 are special norms. There is a reason for making this division. Not all doubtful rescripts are to be interpreted according to the norms of canons 50 and 68. The regulations laid down in these two canons are applicable only in special cases of doubt, namely, when every other means of arriving at the clear meaning of a rescript has been utilized, and doubt remains as to whether a strict or broad interpretation should be given. Therefore, they are special norms. A discussion of these special norms will be reserved for Part III. The present section, or Part II, will be devoted to a consideration of the general norms for the interpretation of rescripts. Chapter III will be concerned with the primary norm; Chapter IV with the secondary norms; and Chapter V will treat of the negative norms. For the most part the chapters will offer a commentary, with historical notes, on canons 49 and 67. Not all of the general norms for the interpretation of rescripts are included by the legislator in these two canons. There is no mention made of the secondary norms. They are understood, however, and must be included in any treatise on the interpretation of rescripts.

CHAPTER III

The Primary Norm

Rescripta intelligenda sunt secundum propriam verborum significationem et communem loquendi usum,...[1]

The purpose of interpretation in regard to rescripts is to discover the mind or intention of the one who issues the rescript. Therefore, the primary concern of the one who interprets a rescript should be to find out what the author of the rescript had in mind at the time he issued his reply. What the author of a rescript has in mind in a particular reply can be discovered in a number of ways. It is not necessary to point out all the ways and means at this moment. Most of them will be mentioned and discussed at one time or another in this and the following chapters. One of them, the primary and principal means, will be the subject of the discussion in the present chapter.

To discover the mind or intention of the author of a rescript is to find out the meaning of the rescript. The primary and principal means for arriving at the meaning of a rescript is through the words which are used to convey the reply. This follows from the very nature of a rescript. A rescript is a written reply in which an ecclesiastical superior makes known his mind or intention relative to a particular request. The will of the superior in the matter is manifested by the words of the rescript. These are the principal means chosen by him to reveal his intentions. Therefore, to interpret a rescript is nothing more than to inquire into and determine the will of the superior as expressed in the written words which go to make up the reply. In order to determine the will of the superior, then, one should look, first of all, to the words of the rescript.

An important thing, of course, is to read the rescript. A superficial glance at the text of the rescript is not enough. It should

[1] Can. 49.

be read carefully. This may seem like a foregone conclusion and hardly worth mentioning here. It is no exaggeration, however, to say that a great many of the doubts which arise in connection with rescripts are caused by a careless and too hurried reading of the text.

ARTICLE I. THE IMPORTANCE OF THE WORDS

So important are the words of a rescript that, unless it is clear that the author of a rescript intends otherwise, one may never depart from the meaning conveyed by them. This is but an application of a fundamental principle of jurisprudence which ordains, that in the interpretation of any legal document one must, first of all, go back to the meaning of the words. The principle is clearly enunciated in the precept of Roman Law relative to the interpretation of the terminology of a testament. According to a law in the Digest, the meaning of the words of a testament must be adhered to unless it is clear that the testator intended otherwise.[2]

The same principle is found in Decretal Law. In a letter to the Bishop of Amiens, Pope Alexander III (1159-1181) instructed the Bishop that, if he wished to know for certain which privileges of exemption the Knights of the Temple and the Knights Hospitallers enjoyed in his diocese, he should examine the letters containing their privileges and observe what he found in them. The Pope added that he wished the Knights to observe the tenor of their privileges, so that they would appear in no way to exceed their limits.[3] The gloss to this chapter notes that privileges are to be inspected in order to find out what they contain. They are to be observed according to what they state, and one should not depart

---

[2] "Non aliter a significatione verborum recedi oportet, quam cum manifestum est aliud sensisse testatorem."—D. (32.1) 67—*Corpus Iuris Civilis* (3 vols., Berolini, 1928-1929)—Vol. I *Digesta,* quae recognovit T. Mommsen et retractavit P. Kreuger (ed. stereotypa 15).

[3] C. 7, X, *de privilegiis et excessibus privilegiatorum,* V, 33—*Decretales D. Gregorii Papae IX una Cum Glossis Restitutae* (Romae, 1582); Jaffé, *Regesta Pontificum Romanorum ab condita Ecclesia ad annum post Christum natum* MCXCVIII, ed. 2 correctam et auctam auspiciis G. Wattenbach, curaverunt S. Loewenfeld, F. Kaltenbrunner, P. Ewald (2 vols., Lipsiae, 1885-1888), n. 11866.

from the "form" of the words.[4] In stating that one is not to depart from the "form" of the words, the glossator refers to the law of the Digest mentioned in the previous paragraph. Although the law speaks only of a testament, nevertheless, the glossator cites it as applying to privileges. The idea is that one is not to depart from the meaning of the words of a letter conveying a privilege unless it is certain that the one who grants the favor intends otherwise.[5]

The principle, as a norm for the interpretation of privileges, is included in the legislation of the Code. In Canon 67 the legislator uses almost the same words as Pope Alexander in his letter to the Bishop of Amiens. The canon directs that a privilege is to be understood according to the tenor (meaning) of its words.[6] The rule is designed to cover the interpretation of all privileges. Of interest here is the fact that it applies to rescripts that grant privileges. Actually, all rescripts are subject to the same rule of interpretation.[7]

ARTICLE II. THE PROPER MEANING OF WORDS AS THE PRIMARY NORM FOR INTERPRETATION

A rescript should be interpreted, first of all, according to the meaning of the words. Since words do not always have the same meaning, it becomes necessary at times to determine which meaning of the words is intended by the superior in a rescript. The primary and principal norm to be followed in order to arrive at the meaning of the words of a rescript is but an application of the primary and principal norm for all interpretation. Rescripts are to be understood according to the proper meaning of their terms.

As a general rule, the words of any legal document should be understood according to the proper meaning of the words. This is brought out by one of the civil law glossators, Accursius

---

[4] *Glossa ordinaria* ad c. 7, X, *de privilegiis et excessibus privilegiatorum*, V, 33, s.v. *Ex inspectione.*

[5] ". . . a forma verborum sine certa scientia non est recedendum."—*Glossa ordinaria* ad c. 12, X, de decimis, III, 30, s.v. *Intelligeremus.*

[6] "Privilegium ex ipsius tenore aestimandum est, . . ."

[7] Reiffenstuel, *Jus Canonicum Universum,* lib. I, tit. III, n. 119.

(+ 1260), in his gloss on the law of the Digest concerning the interpretation of the terminology of a testament. As mentioned before, the law states that one is not to depart from the meaning of the words of a testament, unless it is clear that the testator intends otherwise.[8] In his gloss to the law, Accursius suggests that the meaning which is of more frequent use (*magis usitata*) is to be understood in the testament.[9] As will be seen, the meaning which is of more frequent use is referred to as the proper meaning of a word. Cardinal Tuschus (+ 1620) cites the same law in support of his contention that in the field of law words are to be understood in their proper, true, and natural signification.[10] In his treatise on the interpretation of law, Suarez maintains that in the interpretation of any human law one must, first of all, go back to the proper meaning of the words, for it is upon this that the interpretation of law largely depends. He adds that, unless there is some obstacle in the way, the proper meaning of the words is always to be preferred as a means, or norm, for interpreting a law.[11]

The same rule holds true in regard to the interpretation of rescripts. In the very beginning of his discussion of the interpretation of rescripts, Reiffenstuel lays down the rule that, generally speaking, where the words of a rescript are clear, they are to be understood and interpreted according to their proper meaning and the *communem usum loquendi.*[12] The legislator of the Code uses almost the same words in Canon 49, when he declares that rescripts are to be understood according to the proper meaning of the words and the *communem loquendi usum.*

Before discussing various aspects of the rule in relation to rescripts, a brief consideration of the proper meaning of words and the *communis loquendi usus* is in order.

---

[8] D. (32.1) 67.

[9] Glossa, s.v. *A significatione.*

[10] "Verba sunt interpretanda secundum propriam significationem . . . quia semper debent intelligi proprie, vere, et naturaliter. . . ."—*Practicae Conclusiones Iuris in omni foro frequentiores* (5 vols., Lugduni, 1634), VIII, Litt. V, Concl. 91, nn. 3-6 (hereafter cited *Practicae Conclusiones*).

[11] *De Legibus,* lib. VI, c. 1, n. 7.

[12] *Jus Canonicum Universum,* lib. I, tit. III, n. 119.

ARTICLE III. THE PROPER MEANING OF WORDS AND THE *Communis Loquendi Usus*

In a canon of the IV Lateran Council (1215), Pope Innocent III (1198-1216) decreed that no one could be summoned, by means of Apostolic Letters, before a judge who was more than two days' journey (*ultra duas dietas*) away from the diocese of the one summoned, unless both parties consented to it, or the letter expressly mentioned that the decree of the council did not hold.[13] This canon was later incorporated into the decretal collection of Pope Gregory IX (1227-1241).[14]

The glossator to the canon asks whether the word *"dieta"* should be understood in its usual sense according to the custom of the region, or whether it should be understood in its legal, or technical, sense of 20 thousand paces. He is of the opinion that it should be understood according to its usual meaning, namely, "a day's journey." The reason for this interpretation, he adds, is that names are to be understood according to their common usage.[15]

In support of his position, the glossator cites a law of the Digest in which there is stated: "names are not to be understood according to the opinion of individuals but according to their common usage."[16] In connection with this law there is a rather lengthy discussion as to the proper meaning of the word *"supellex."* The historical development of the meaning of the word is considered, and a negative definition of the term is given.[17] The meaning of the word is of no particular interest here. Important, however, is the principle upon which the meaning of the term is determined. According to the principle, as given in the Law of the Digest mentioned above, the meaning of a word is derived from usage and is not subject to the mere choice of an individual.

---

[13] C. 37—Hardouin, *Acta Conciliorum et Epistolae Decretales ac Constitutiones Summorum Pontificum* (11 vols. in 12, Parisiis, 1714), vol. VII, 47 (hereafter cited *Hardouin*).

[14] C. 28, X, *de rescriptis,* I, 3.

[15] *Glossa ordinaria,* s.v. *Ultra duas dietas.*

[16] ". . . non enim ex opinionibus singulorum sed ex communi usu nomina exaudiri debent."—D. (33.10) 7, 2.

[17] The word means furniture or household furnishings: "Supellex est domesticum patris familias instrumentum quod neque argento aurove facto vel vesti adnumeretur."—D. (33.10) 1.

This position is easy to see, for if the meaning of words were left up to the individual using them, the exchange of ideas would become all but impossible. As it is, a word is given a particular meaning, and through repeated usage the signification attached to that word becomes the commonly accepted meaning. Current social usage, then, ordinarily, determines the way in which words are to be understood. The meaning which is sanctioned by common usage is referred to as the proper meaning of a term.[18]

Section 1. Different Proper Meanings

There is a certain latitude within the proper meaning of words. The proper signification of a word may change, or the same word may have a number of proper meanings. Authors generally distinguish between the *natural,* the *usual* and the *juridical* proper meaning of terms.[19] The *natural* meaning of a word is the one that is usually first given to a word and the one that ordinarily represents things as they are in nature.[20] In many cases the natural meaning of a word will be the proper meaning of that term. This is true, however, only as long as the natural meaning remains commonly accepted and understood among men. The natural proper signification of a term may be confirmed by usage, or it may be modified by the use which it receives. The modified use of the term will then prevail.[21] Where the natural meaning of a word is not

[18] Accursius, *Glossa* ad D. (33.10) 7, 2, s.v. *Ex communi usu.* For a consideration of the proper meaning of words with more complete references cf. Schmidt, *op. cit.,* pp. 127-131. According to Suarez, the proper meaning of words: "imprimis sumenda est ex usitata significatione, vel communi usu. . . ."—*De Legibus,* lib. VIII, c. 28, n. 16. According to Michiels, "Significatio verbi propria generatim loquendo ea est, quae adaequate respondet conceptui ad quem exprimendum verbum illud fuit institutum, quaeque regulariter verbo illi, quando usitatur, sub-ponitur."—*Normae Generales,* I, 517-518.

[19] Cf. Suarez, *op. cit.,* lib. IV, c. 1, n. 9; Van Hove, *De Legibus,* n. 252; Michiels, *loc. cit.*

[20] "Naturalis significatio orta est ex primaeva impositione nominis diversis rebus, qua res significari solent prout occurrunt in rerum natura et naturaliter sunt. Ita filii intelliguntur naturales non adoptivi, mors intelligitur naturalis non civilis, familia naturalis non religiosa."—Van Hove, *loc. cit.*

[21] "Et plus statur usui quam significationi vocis. . . . Imo usui statur contra naturam vocis."—*Glossa ordinaria* ad c. 28, X, *de rescriptis,* I, 3, s.v. *Ultra duas dietas;* cf. can. 29.

entirely changed by the subsequent use which it receives, then it, too, is to be considered as a proper meaning of that term.

The *usual* meaning of a word is, as the name implies, the one that derives from usage. Common usage, or the *communis loquendi usus,* is the most important single factor in determining the proper meaning of a word. Of all the proper meanings that a word may have, the one that is confirmed by repeated usage is to be looked upon as the most proper.[22] The *usual,* or common, meaning of a word does not necessarily exclude the natural, figurative or even the juridical meaning of that term. As Accursius notes, the figurative meaning of a word can become its usual meaning.[23] Among canonists, the juridical meaning of a word may be looked upon as the usual meaning for them.[24]

The *usual* meaning is the one that, here and now, is the commonly understood meaning of that word. In order to determine the *usual* meaning of a word in a particular situation, it will often be necessary not only to consider the person who is using the word, but also the ordinary, common meaning of the term in the region where the person is located. The meaning attached to a word may be common only within a certain area, and then it is peculiar to that region. It may be common outside of that region, and, if used by all men, then it becomes the universally accepted proper meaning. In either case the meaning is *usual.* In the first case, however, the meaning attached to the word is *usual,* or common, only within a restricted territory.

The meaning of a particular word may be considered as *usual* only for a limited class of persons in a certain profession. Thus, some words are given a technical or legal meaning which is altogether different from the general understanding of these terms. What would be an unusual meaning for the general populace becomes the *usual* and accepted meaning for the scientist or the lawyer. In this way the juridical meaning becomes the usual one.

---

[22] "Sensus enim verborum apprime determinatur communi hominum usu, ideoque significatio *usualis* vel communis est maxime propria."—Van Hove, *op. cit.,* n. 252.

[23] *Glossa* ad D. (33.10) 7, 2, s.v. *Ex communi usu.*

[24] "Usualis significatio vocatur iuridica, si haec usu iuris peritorum vel definitione iuris ipsius est determinata."—Van Hove, *loc. cit.*

A few brief comments may be noted in regard to the *juridical,* or legal, proper meaning of words. At times the signification of a term is determined by the use which it receives among those learned in the law. At other times its meaning is set down in the law itself. In either case, the word takes on a certain legal connotation which then becomes the usual and proper meaning of that term in matters of law. Since any meaning of a word that is sanctioned by common usage is to be considered as a proper meaning of that term, then, where a word acquires a particular legal signification as a result of repeated use among jurists, the legal meaning of that term is to be numbered among its proper meanings. Where the meaning of a word is determined by law, then that meaning of the term must be adhered to in all matters covered by the law in question. The law antecedently, as it were, prescribes the meaning that must be accepted, and therefore predetermines the proper meaning of the term as far as the law is concerned.[25] Thus, the Code of Canon Law determines the juridic proper meaning of certain terms and expressions.[26]

Section 2. The Improper Meaning of Words

At times words may have to be understood in an improper sense. The improper meaning of a term is something other than the natural, common or juridical proper signification. It is an unusual one, in the sense that an improper meaning is not a commonly accepted meaning that has been approved and accepted by usage. Instead, it depends upon the intention of the person who uses it.[27] On occasion, a person may give his own meaning to a term, e.g., in a will. When the use of the term involves a de-

---

[25] "Si ius in aliquo loco interpretatur vocabulum, illa dicitur propria significatio."—Tuschus, *Practicae Conclusiones,* VIII, Litt. V, Concl. 91, n. 28.

[26] For example, *ordinarius,* in can. 198; *sacra ordinatio,* in can. 950; *beneficium ecclesiasticum* in can. 1409. Can. 488 gives a long list of canonical definitions.

[27] "Significatio verbi impropria per oppositionem ea dicitur, quae neque juridice neque usualiter neque naturaliter verbo convenit, sed a loquente, pro speciali suo lubitu vel saltem ob rationes sibi visas, verbo substituitur";—Michiels, *op. cit.,* I, 519.

parture from its proper or usual acceptation, then the word is said to be used in an improper sense.

ARTICLE IV. RESCRIPTS MUST BE UNDERSTOOD ACCORDING TO THE PROPER MEANING OF THE WORDS AND THE *Communem Loquendi Usum*

So far it has been pointed out that the purpose of interpretation in regard to rescripts is to discover the mind or intention of the superior who issues the rescript. In order to achieve this objective, one should begin by considering the words which are used to make known this intention.[28] So important are the words that one may never depart from their meaning, unless it is certain that the superior who issues the rescript clearly intends otherwise. Progressing a step further, one must note that as a general rule the words of any legal document are to be understood according to their proper meaning. The same rule is to be applied to rescripts.[29] In fact, canon 49 prescribes that rescripts are to be understood according to the proper meaning of the words and the *communem loquendi usum*. Before it could be shown how the rule applied, it was necessary to give some explanation of the proper meaning of words. With the idea of the proper meaning of words in mind, then, it remains to be seen how the rule operates as the primary and principal norm for the interpretation of rescripts.

Section 1. Rescripts Subject to the Norm

In his treatise on the interpretation of rescripts, Reiffenstuel begins by stating that when the words of a rescript are clear, they

[28] ". . . quia verba sunt quae ex intentione legislatoris potissimum assumuntur ad declarandam voluntatem suam, ergo illo etiam primo et principaliter consuli debent ad eamdem voluntatem cognoscendam."—Suarez, *De Legibus,* lib. VI, c. 1, n. 16.

[29] "Quemadmodum igitur in legibus et in testamentis debemus ex verbis inquirere voluntatem legislatoris et testatoris; ita pariter ex verbis debemus arguere voluntatem rescribentis, et ex verbis non utcumque sumptis, sed secundum propriam verborum significationem et communem loquendi usum."—Ojetti, *Commentarium in Codicem Iuris Canonici* (4 vols., Romae: Apud Aedes Universitatis Gregorianae, 1927-1931), I, 246 (hereafter cited *Commentarium*).

are to be understood and interpreted according to their proper meaning and the *communem usum loquendi.*[30] What he has to say is true, as will be seen more clearly in the course of this discussion. However, his statement tends to obscure a very important fact in regard to the norm which he advocates. The fact is, that all rescripts are subject to this norm. An initial attempt must be made to understand all rescripts according to the proper meaning of their terms and the *communem loquendi usum.*[31] Only after the directions laid down in the norm have been followed, can one begin to conclude whether the terms of a rescript are clear or doubtful. The norm is designed to bring out clearly the meaning intended in a rescript and is not to be applied only when the words of a rescript are clear, as might be inferred from Reiffenstuel's statement. It is to be applied to each and every rescript as the first and foremost means of revealing its contents. That is why it is referred to as the primary and principal norm for the interpretation of rescripts.

Ordinarily, the application of the norm will disclose that the meaning of a rescript is clear. After following its prescriptions, there will usually be no doubt as to the intention of the author. The rule was formulated with this very idea in mind. It is to be expected that the author of a rescript will make every reasonable effort to be clear. In order to be clear, he must use words that will be able to be understood. As a general rule the words of a language are used in their ordinary, usual sense, i.e., according to their proper meaning. If this were not so, then the interchange of ideas would become fraught with all sorts of difficulties. Doubts and uncertainties would arise, and each one would be left free to use and understand words in an arbitrary fashion. Therefore, in order to be understood, the author of a rescript must use words according to their proper meaning. From the law of the Code it would seem that he has an obligation to do so, for the legislator would not decree that rescripts are to be understood according to the

---

[30] *Jus Canonicum Universum,* lib. I, tit. III, n. 119.

[31] "Secundum sensum proprium verborum et secundum communem loquendi usum omnia rescripta, etiam quae concedunt privilegia et dispensationes, intelligenda sunt."—Van Hove, *De Rescriptis,* n. 221.

proper meaning of the words unless there were a corresponding duty on the part of the superior who issues the rescript to use such a meaning.[32] By understanding a rescript according to the proper meaning of its terms, then, there is every reason to suppose that the inherent clarity of the text will be revealed, and that is why an initial effort should be made to understand all rescripts according to the prescriptions of the primary norm.

Section 2. The Application of the Norm

Once the primary norm has been applied to a rescript and its meaning becomes clear, no further investigation is necessary, nor permissible. There becomes applicable immediately the well known axiom: *"Verba clara non admittunt interpretationem neque voluntatis coniecturam."*[33] Where the meaning of the words of a rescript are clear, the need for interpretation ceases.

In applying the primary norm, however, some investigation may be necessary in order to determine the clear meaning of the words. As noted in a previous article, a word may have more than one proper meaning.[34] When this occurs in a rescript, it becomes necessary to find out, as nearly as possible, the proper meaning intended by the author. The author of a rescript can have only one meaning in mind when he issues his reply.

Canon 49 directs that the words of a rescript are to be understood according to their proper meaning and the *communem loquendi usum.* Notice should be taken of the fact that the legislator

---

[32] Reiffenstuel argues in a similar vein with respect to the interpretation of law. After stating that the words of a law are to be understood according to their proper signification, he adds: "Accedit ratio: quia legislator debet uti verbis manifestis, seu claris in editione legis, ne aliquid per obscuritatem in captionem contineat . . . ergo is etiam debet uti verbis in significatione propria, ac proinde haec secundum propriam significationem intelligi; alioquin nihil firmum stabiliretur, sed omnia forent plena cavillationibus."—*op. cit.*, lib. I, tit. II, n. 390. Cf. also Suarez, *op. cit.*, lib. VI, c. 1, nn. 7, 8.

[33] Reiffenstuel, *op. cit.*, lib. I, tit. II, n. 384. Another version of the same axiom is as follows: "Ubi verba non sunt ambigua, non est locus interpretationi";—*Glossa ordinaria* ad c. 8, *de consuetudinibus,* X, I, 4, s.v. *Iuri Communi.*

[34] Cf. *supra,* pp. 56-58.

does not say simply proper meaning, but proper meaning and the *communem loquendi usum.* By *communis loquendi usus* is meant the common manner of speaking, or, more succinctly, common usage. By adding the phrase, the legislator makes it clear that the use which a term receives must be taken into consideration along with any other proper meaning that it may have. The phrase could have been omitted without altering the sense of the canon, for the meaning of a term that is sanctioned by common usage is always looked upon as a proper meaning of that term.[35]

As pointed out earlier, the proper meaning of words is determined to a great extent by the manner in which they are used.[36] In fact, that meaning is to be considered most proper which is confirmed by repeated use.[37] As a general rule, then, the terms of a rescript should be understood according to their common, every-day meaning.

Often enough the commonly accepted meaning of a term will correspond to its use in law. This is not always the case, of course, and in matters of law, where there is opposition between the ordinary, every-day meaning of a term and its acceptance in law, the legal meaning will be preferred. A rescript is a legal document in which all manner of legal, canonical subjects are dealt with. The terminology of a rescript will almost always have a legal connotation. If the terms in a rescript have a juridic as well as a common, ordinary proper meaning, then the former must be given prior consideration.[38]

The *communis loquendi usus* of canon 49 offers no real contradiction to this statement. The phrase does not mean that a rescript must always be understood according to the common, every-day meaning of terms. Hence it does not exclude the possibility of

---

[35] "Communis loquendi modus, quem can. 49 expresse memorat, est species quaedam contenta in genere sensus proprii verborum quae, in canone 18 circa interpretationem legis, expressa non est, continetur tamen in formula generali sensus proprii."—Van Hove, *De Rescriptis,* n. 221.

[36] Cf. *supra,* pp. 55, 56.

[37] ". . . significatio propria praeprimis habenda est significatio per 'communem loquendi usum' firmata."—Michiels, *Normae Generales,* II, 423.

[38] "In rescriptis intelligendis semper est adhibendus sensus proprius, praeprimis sensus iuridicus. . . ."—Van Hove, *loc. cit.*

interpreting a rescript according to some other proper meaning, in particular, the juridic proper signification of terms.[39] In fact, the juridic meaning is the meaning commonly used in law and in legal matters. For, in matters of law the legal meaning of a word becomes the commonly accepted meaning of that term for those who have to deal with the law. Therefore, in a legal document such as a rescript the juridic proper meaning of a term is necessarily included within the *communis loquendi usus* of the ecclesiastical superior who grants it.

The juridic proper meaning of a term may be defined in the law. Where such is the case, one should look to the law for the correct understanding of the word. A word may also achieve a legal meaning through usage. Of particular importance in this regard is the *stylus curiae* from which a rescript emanates. Through the repeated observance of procedural rules and customs in a particular curia, the same words tend to be used over and over again. In the course of time, some may take on a special meaning that is peculiar to that curia. As a result, rescripts from the respective curias will have to be understood according to the meaning of words currently in use in each curia. Particular attention should be paid to any use of terms that is peculiar to the various Congregations, Tribunals and Offices of the Roman Curia.[40]

The juridic proper meaning of a term may also be determined by the use which it receives among those learned in the law. Such a meaning should not be ignored in examining the words of a rescript. If a legal term has achieved general acceptance among authors and canonists, there is no reason why the author of a rescript can not use it according to that meaning, for by usage the legal term becomes the usual term and as a result is considered to be the *communis loquendi usus*.

Where there is no conflict between a juridical and the common,

---

[39] "Communis autem loquendi modus hic non exprimitur ad excludendos alios sensus proprios, nominatim sensum iuridicum verborum."—Van Hove, *loc. cit.*

[40] "In rescriptis intelligendis semper est adhibendus sensus proprius, praeprimis sensus iuridicus, qui vel per ipsam iuris dispositionem definitur, . . . vel per stylum Curiae Romanae determinatur."—Van Hove, *loc. cit.* Cf. also Schmalzgrueber, *Jus Ecclesiasticum Universum,* lib. I, tit. III, n. 24.

every-day meaning of a term, the latter should be considered as the proper meaning intended by the author, for they are synonymous. Even here, however, there may be need for investigation. In nearly every rescript, certain terms will have a universally accepted common proper meaning. Such terms should present no problem as far as interpretation is concerned. It is possible, however, that some words or expressions will be common only in the place where the author of the rescript is located. They may have a somewhat different import in the place where the rescript is received. In that case the particular usage that prevails in the locality of the author will most likely decide the meaning that he has in mind.[41] Thus the usual meaning of a term in Rome may be quite different from the meaning that is common in some other part of the world.[42]

If the commonly accepted meaning of a term does not seem to give a clear indication of what the author of a rescript has in mind, then one may turn to the natural proper meaning, which may differ in some degree from the most commonly understood meaning of the term. One or the other of the proper meanings mentioned so far should serve to reveal the author's intention. Due to limitations inherent in any language, there may be times when the author will have to depart somewhat from the usual meaning of a term. This will be the exception rather than the rule. Since there is a certain latitude within the proper meaning of words, it may prove difficult at times to decide which meaning is most apt to be the clearest. Comparative examination on the basis of the various proper meanings, conducted according to the juridic principles outlined in this section, should help to alleviate these difficulties.

Context

No attempt should be made to understand the words of a rescript apart from their context. The context as well as the text should be

[41] "Communis loquendi usus autem praeprimis intelligitur communis ipsius rescribentis loquendi usus. . . ."—Michiels, *op. cit.*, II, 423.

[42] On this point Vermeersch-Creusen note: "Cum agitur de rescriptis romanis, utile erit Urbis usus cognoscere. Sic vox Collegii Romae significationem habet quae trans Alpes ignoratur, cum applicetur quoque ad conservatoria puellarum."—*Epitome,* I, n. 165.

noted. Canon 18 makes specific mention of the context in regard to the interpretation of laws.[43] No mention of the context is made in canon 49. It does not follow from this omission, however, that one need only care about the words of a rescript as they appear in the text. The text and context together help to convey the proper meaning of the words and, hence, the intention of the author.[44]

It is not enough to know the proper meaning of terms only in their immediate text. Their context must be considered at the same time. Where a word has more than one proper meaning, it is only from the context in which it is used that one can begin to determine what meaning is intended. Thus, the term *"ius"* may denote the right that belongs to a person, or the norm by which that right is determined by law. In order to establish with certainty which of the two meanings is intended in a particular case, it will be necessary to consider the context in which it is used.

According to a dictum of Roman Law, to interpret a part of a law without considering the whole law is the mark of a barbarian:

> Incivile est nisi tota lege perspecta una aliqua particula eius proposita iudicare et respondere.[45]

The same idea is present as the basis for the principle of law enunciated in one of the decretals of Gregory IX:

> Propterea si prolixam epistolam ad interpretandum accipere fortasse contigerit, rogo non verbum ex verbo, sed sensum ex sensu transferre: quia dum proprietas verborum attenditur, sensus veritatis amittitur.[46]

---

[43] "Leges ecclesiasticae intelligendae sunt secundum propriam verborum significationem in textu et contextu consideratam."

[44] "Scilicet rescriptum est id, quod voluit superior rescribens; voluntas autem alicuius manifestatur per verba prout sonant, in textu et contextu considerata, ut dicitur in canone 18."—Ojetti, *op. cit.*, I, 246.

[45] D. (1.3) 24.

[46] C. 8, X, *de verborum significatione,* V, 40.

CHAPTER IV

Secondary Norms

The previous chapter was devoted to a discussion of the primary norm for the interpretation of rescripts. In the beginning of the chapter, it was noted that the purpose of interpretation in regard to rescripts is to discover the mind or intention of the superior who grants a rescript. The principal means for accomplishing this purpose is the use of the primary norm. The proper meaning of the words and the *communis loquendi usus* will usually reveal the meaning intended in a rescript. This is true so long as the meaning of the words is thereby made clear, and there is no indication that the author of the rescript intends otherwise.

The present chapter will be concerned with the secondary norms for the interpretation of rescripts. Its object will be to discuss what course of action must be followed in the event that the meaning of the words of a rescript remains doubtful after the application of the primary norm. Such an eventuality is possible in view of the fact that the proper meaning of terms may sometimes remain obscure or equivocal. A term may have several commonly accepted meanings, so that it becomes difficult to determine with certainty which meaning is intended by the author of a rescript.[1] When such a situation develops, it becomes necessary to use additional means in order to discover the mind or intention of the author. Such means may be referred to as secondary, or subsidiary norms for the interpretation of rescripts.[2]

---

[1] "*Sed quid si significatio verborum propria vere obscura seu aequivoca sit,* seu ex communi loquendi usu de pluribus intelligi queat quae aeque probabiliter videntur a legislatore volita?"—Michiels, *Normae Generales,* II, 428.

[2] The terms "secondary" and "subsidiary" are used mainly by authors in connection with the interpretation of law. "Si per examen verborum legis, quacumque ex causa, significatio eorum clara ac certa non redditur, ad interpretationem obtinendam modo subsidiario 'ad locos Codicis parallelos, si qui sint, ad legis finem ac circumstantias et ad mentem legislatoris est recurrendum' (c. 18). Haec sunt normae subsidiariae";—Brems, "De Inter-

ARTICLE I. THE EXISTENCE OF SUCH NORMS

Canon 49 makes no mention of secondary norms for the interpretation of rescripts. The first part of the canon contains the primary norm for their interpretation, and the second part contains a negative norm prohibiting the extension of rescripts to cases not expressed in them.[3] There is no provision in the canon for the use of secondary norms as is found in canon 18 for the interpretation of laws. The first part of canon 18 directs that ecclesiastical laws are to be understood according to the proper meaning of the terms as found in the text and context.[4] This is the primary norm for the interpretation of law and is identical to the primary norm for the interpretation of rescripts as given in canon 49, although the wording in the two canons is somewhat different. The second section of canon 18 declares that if the words of a law remain doubtful (after the application of the primary norm), then recourse must be had to parallel passages of the Code, if there are any, to the end and the circumstances of the law, and to the mind of the legislator.[5]

In canon 18, then, the legislator takes cognizance of the fact that the primary norm for interpretation may sometimes fail to bring out clearly the meaning intended in a law. Doubts and obscurities may remain despite all efforts to understand a law according to the proper meaning of its words by the use of only the primary norm. Therefore, he gives a list of other means, or norms that must be resorted to in an effort to clear up the doubts and uncertainties.[6]

---

pretatione Authentica Codicis J. C. per Pont. Commissionem," *Jus Pontificium,* XV (1935), 302. Van Hove refers to the same norms in canon 18 as secondary norms.—*De Legibus,* n. 249. The same terminology may be applied to the interpretation of rescripts.

[3] "Rescripta intelligenda sunt secundum propriam verborum significationem et communem loquendi usum, nec debent ad casus alios praeter expressos extendi."

[4] "Leges ecclesiasticae intelligendae sunt secundum propriam verborum significationem in textu et contextu consideratam."

[5] ". . . quae si dubia et obscura manserit, ad locos Codicis parallelos, si qui sint, ad legis finem ac circumstantias et ad mentem legislatoris est recurrendum."

[6] Cf. Schmidt, *The Principles of Authentic Interpretation,* p. 138.

There seems to be some disagreement as to whether there are similar secondary and subsidiary norms for the interpretation of rescripts, or whether the primary norm alone must suffice before invoking the special norms of canon 50. According to Beste, it would seem that the primary norm must suffice. He states in no uncertain terms, that in the interpretation of rescripts recourse must not be had to the subsidiary norms for interpretation as given in canon 18 for laws, but that the words of a rescript must be taken *prout sonant.*[7] He gives no reasons for the statement which he makes. In taking exception to what Beste has to say, this writer does not mean to imply that the very same secondary norms that are set down by the legislator in canon 18 for laws are to be followed in the interpretation of rescripts. Canon 18 is concerned only with laws and not with rescripts. However, as Michiels notes, the norms for the interpretation of rescripts are but applications, with certain modifications, of the general principles which govern the interpretation of law.[8] With due consideration of the modifications that may be necessary, it will be seen that the secondary norms for the interpretation of laws have their counterpart in the interpretation of rescripts. Beste's statement seems to imply that there are no such secondary norms for rescripts.

It must be admitted that the majority of modern authors make no mention of secondary norms when discussing the interpretation of rescripts. In commenting on canon 49, most of them merely point out the fact that rescripts are to be understood according to the proper meaning of the words and the *communem loquendi usum.* They give some explanation of the proper meaning of words and discuss the importance of the *communis loquendi usus.* When the question of doubt arises, they immediately refer to canon 50 which has to do with the strict and broad interpretation of doubtful rescripts.[9] There are some authors, however, who mention specifically other norms or means that should be used to clarify the tenor

---

[7] *Introductio in Codicem,* p. 115.

[8] *Op. cit.,* II, 422.

[9] Cf. Abbo-Hannon, *Sacred Canons,* p. 81; Badiï, *Institutiones Iuris Canonici* (3. ed., 2 vols., Florentiae, 1921, 1922), pp. 68, 69; Cappello, *Summa Iuris Canonici,* I, 123; Cicognani, *Canon Law,* pp. 735-739; Coronata, *Institutiones,* I, n. 71; Ojetti, *Commentarium,* I, 245-247.

of the document before one can definitely conclude that the words of a rescript are doubtful.[10] According to O'Neill, "Whenever, at first sight, the meaning of a word or expression in a rescript appears doubtful, the ordinary means proposed in can. 18 for the interpretation of doubtful laws may be employed in determining the exact content of the rescript."[11] Michiels goes still further and states that all the means of interpretation should be used, even those which are extrinsic to a rescript or complementary to the norms expressed in canon 18.[12]

Before discussing in any detail the rules which the above-mentioned authors give, it should be noted that similar rules are found among certain pre-Code canonists, mainly in connection with their treatment of the interpretation of privileges.[13] Suarez, in fact, appears to be the main source for most of the rules that are given. At the conclusion of his treatise on the interpretation of privileges, he gives a short summary in which he outlines the practice to be observed in their interpretation. He indicates first of all, that when the words of a privilege are clear enough, and their meaning is certain, then no interpretation is to be attempted, but the tenor or form of the privilege is to be observed. However, when the words are in any way ambiguous, then one must strive before all else to determine by all possible means the intention of the one granting the privilege. The reason for this, he adds, is that the worth of a privilege depends wholly upon the will of the author. He then proceeds to give a list of five aids or norms that may be

---

[10] Michiels, *op. cit.*, II, 428; O'Neill, *Papal Rescripts of Favor*, pp. 102, 103; Regatillo, *Institutiones Iuris Canonici* (2. ed., 2 vols., Santander: Sal Terrae, 1946), I, 97 (hereafter cited *Institutiones*); Roelker, *Principles of Privilege*, pp. 77-79.

[11] *Loc. cit.*

[12] "Imprimis sane adhibenda sunt omnia interpretationis adminicula, etiam illa quae sunt ipsi rescripto extranea seu regularum in can. 18 expressarum completoria, ut proprius sensus, ex inspectione rescripti obscurus, pro posse enucleetur et effectiva concedentis intentio cum certitudine determinetur." —*loc. cit.*

[13] Grandclaude, *Jus Canonicum juxta Ordinem Decretalium* (5 vols. in 3, Parisiis, 1883), lib. V, sec. III, n. 1 (hereafter cited *Jus Canonicum*); Schmalzgrueber, *Jus Ecclesiasticum Universum*, lib. V, tit. XXXIII, n. 118; Suarez, *De Legibus*, lib. VIII, c. 28, n. 19.

used in seeking to determine the mind or intention of the author of a privilege.[14]

The rules which Suarez gives for the interpretation of privileges are in reality rules for the interpretation of rescripts. It is evident from the very first rule that he gives, that he is speaking principally of privileges that are granted by means of a rescript, for he states that one should look first of all to the petition in order to ascertain the intention of the grantor.[15]

The following article will contain a discussion of the various secondary norms for the interpretation of rescripts. In the course of the discussion it will be seen that most of the norms mentioned are but applications of the secondary norms for the interpretation of laws as prescribed in canon 18. The fact that the legislator does not enumerate these norms in the title on rescripts does not prove that they are not to be employed as means for arriving at a correct understanding of the contents of a rescript. Various means in addition to the primary norm are to be used in the interpretation of rescripts. In canon 18 the legislator demands that certain secondary norms be resorted to whenever the primary norm fails to reveal the meaning intended in a law. The Code does not proclaim expressly any such obligatory norms for the interpretation of rescripts. The very nature of legal interpretation, however, demands that every juridically approved norm be employed to comprehend the meaning of the terms of a rescript. Only after such attempts have proved of no avail may one conclude that the words of a rescript are doubtful. Some of the principal means that may be used are those that will now be discussed in the article that follows. These norms are juridically approved for the present purpose in virtue of canon 20, because there is a definite similarity between a law and a rescript.[16]

ARTICLE II. THE INDIVIDUAL NORMS

Section 1. The Petition

If the words of a rescript remain obscure or uncertain after the initial attempt to understand them according to the primary norm,

---

[14] *Op. cit.,* lib. VIII, c. 28, nn. 18, 19.

[15] *Ibid.,* n. 19.

[16] Cf. e.g., can. 17, § 3.

then the doubt can often be solved by comparing the rescript with the petition.[17] Since a rescript is an answer to a petition, the contents of such a reply will be determined to a great extent by what is stated in the request. A petition will usually contain a narration of certain facts, mention of the object of the petition and the reasons why the rescript should be granted. These are what influence the ecclesiastical superior who draws up a rescript. This consideration holds true, of course, only in rescripts that are granted *ad instantiam* or *ad preces.* Since *motu proprio* rescripts are issued for reasons other than those that are set forth in the application, and since the petition is the occasion rather than the cause for granting the rescript, recourse must be had to other norms for their interpretation. In *ad instantiam* rescripts, however, as the terminology suggests, the answer is given at the instance of the petitioner. Therefore, there will usually be close agreement between what is state in the petition and what is contained in the rescript.[18] If a doubt should arise concerning the meaning of the terms of the rescript, then the petition may very well serve as a means of clarification.

This is particularly true where the shorter form is used in a rescript. According to the practice observed in most curias, and especially in the Roman Curia, rescripts are issued in two forms. They are distinguished from each other only by reason of the fact that one form is more detailed and therefore longer than the other. Both forms contain three parts, namely, a narrative part, a motive part and a dispositive part. In the more detailed form, the narrative part recounts or sums up the facts that are mentioned in the petition; the motive part outlines the reasons for granting the rescript; and the dispositive part contains the actual reply in which the law is stated, a favor granted, etc., together with the conditions to be observed. In the shorter form, the narrative part is restricted to the name of the petitioner and his diocese or religious order, etc.; the motive part is stated briefly or omitted entirely; the dispositive part is condensed and very often contains

[17] "Supplicatio est spectanda ad indagandam mentem concedentis."—Suarez, *loc. cit.;* cf. also Roelker, *op. cit.,* p. 78.

[18] Cf. Suarez, *loc. cit.;* Roelker, *loc. cit.*

the clause *"iuxta petita,"* together with any conditions that may have to be observed.[19]

Whenever the shorter form is used and the phrase *"iuxta petita"* is inserted, then one must of necessity look to the petition in order to understand the rescript correctly. Even when the phrase is omitted, the petition will usually have to be consulted, for the rescript itself will mention only what is absolutely necessary.

Section 2. Initium Rescripti

When the longer form is used, the narrative and motive parts of a rescript will occasionally be of help in understanding the dispositive portion, or the main body of the rescript. This norm, or aid, is what Suarez has in mind when he mentions that the *initium* of an indult granting a privilege should be carefully considered, *"quia juxta illud solent adjungi omnia subsequentia."*[20] A narration of the facts and a recounting of the motives are not always necessary in a rescript, as is evidenced by the fact that they are often omitted in the short form.When they are included, they serve as an introduction to the dispositive part that follows. The fact that they are included is an indication of their importance in relation to the answer that is given. The legislator, or superior, would not go to the trouble of restating them unless their importance warranted it. Therefore, they should be taken into consideration in the event that any terms in the dispositive part are not immediately clear. In some rescripts, the motives mentioned by the superior may differ from those that are listed in the petition. If so, the differences should be noted, for the reasons given by the superior would be a valuable source of interpretation. In any case, the *initium*, or opening sections of a rescript, should not be overlooked whenever the longer form is used.

Section 3. The Subject Matter of a Rescript

The subject matter of a rescript may also help to dispel any doubts that may arise concerning the meaning of its terms.[21] Ec-

[19] Cf. Cicognani, *op. cit.*, 699; Van Hove, *De Rescriptis*, n. 89.

[20] *Loc. cit.*

[21] "Praeterea spectanda est materia subjecta: nam ad illam solent verba accommodari. . . ."—Suarez, *op. cit.*, lib. VIII, c. 28, n. 19.

clesiastical superiors tend to be liberal in some matters and rather strict in others. If a rescript contains matter that is usually looked upon as favorable by the superior, then there is likelihood that a broad interpretation is intended, and hence, a doubt may be able to be resolved by recourse to such an interpretation. Where the contents of a rescript are viewed as unfavorable, i.e., as odious or harmful, then in all probability a strict interpretation is intended, and the doubt may be dispelled by interpreting the terms of the rescript strictly.[22]

Strict and broad interpretation are considered in this section only in so far as they may serve as secondary norms capable of rendering doubtful terms clear. Depending upon the subject matter contained in a rescript, one or the other of these two forms of interpretation is demanded by the legislator, whenever there is a doubt that cannot be resolved according to the primary and secondary norms for interpretation.[23] In this capacity they serve as special, rather than secondary, norms for the interpretation of rescripts. The use of strict and broad interpretation as special norms is discussed fully in Part III of the present study.[24]

Section 4. The Law

The law itself may serve as a guide in the interpretation of rescripts. The provisions of a rescript may be according to the law, contrary to the law, or outside the law. When the terms of a rescript *secundum ius* are doubtful, recourse not only may, but should be had to the law as a possible means of clarifying the doubt.

Frequent mention is made of the law as a norm for the interpretation of rescripts *secundum ius* in the *Corpus Iuris Canonici* and in the commentators prior to the Code. In one of his decretal letters, Pope Innocent III (1198-1216) settled certain doubts which had arisen concerning the meaning of a phrase in a rescript, which he had issued previously, by ordering the phrase to be

[22] ". . . praecipue spectandum est an sit materia ambitiosa, vel etiam periculosa, ex qua posset sumi occasio ad multiplicandas lites vel peccata, ut verba coarctentur."—Suarez, *loc. cit.*

[23] Cf. cans. 50, 68, 85.

[24] Cf. *infra*, pp. 106-144.

understood in keeping with the requirements of the law.[25] In his notations in the gloss, the glossator mentions that the letter is an argument to prove that the words of a rescript are to be understood according to the *ius commune.*[26]

The decretalists cite this letter repeatedly as their main source to show that in doubt rescripts are to be interpreted according to the common law. When they speak of rescripts, they have in mind only rescripts in the strict sense, i.e., rescripts that are issued to further the observance of the law, or rescripts *secundum ius.*[27] Commenting on the letter of his predecessor, Pope Innocent IV (1243-1254) states that in rescripts ambiguous words are to be interpreted according to the *ius commune.*[28] Panormitanus goes even further in his commentary and notes that a doubtful rescript ought to be reduced to the common law, even if this has to be done by using an improper meaning of the words of rearranging a phrase.[29] He gives as his reason the fact that a rescript (in the strict sense) is issued to promote the observance of the law and, therefore, should not contain anything contrary to the law. In order that such a rescript may not operate contrary to its nature, he adds, it ought to be interpreted in such a way as not to go against the common law. This rule must be understood, according to him, only in so far as the words are doubtful, for where there is no ambiguity, there is no need for interpretation.[30] Felinus Sandeus (+ 1503), commenting on the same letter, quotes Joannes Andreae (+ 1348) to the effect that all clauses inserted in Apostolic rescripts *secundum ius* receive all the limitations and interpretations which the law receives.[31]

---

[25] C. 18, X, *de rescriptis,* I, 3. Potthast, n. 59.

[26] *Glossa ordinaria,* s.v. *Praecedat.*

[27] In treating of rescripts contrary to the law and outside the law, the early pre-Code authors avoided the use of the term "rescript" and preferred, instead, to use the terms "privilege," "dispensation," *"beneficium,"* etc. Cf. *supra,* pp. 37-40.

[28] *Commentaria,* lib. I, tit. III, n. 2.

[29] Concerning the use of an improper signification under Code law, cf. *infra,* pp. 98-102; 116, footnote n. 27.

[30] *Commentaria,* lib. I, tit. III, c. 18, n. 1.

[31] *Commentaria in V Libros Decretalium* (3 vols., Venetiis, 1570), lib. I, tit. III, c. 18, n. 5 (hereafter cited *Commentaria*).

From the foregoing brief historical notations, it is apparent that the early pre-Code authors were aware of the value of the law as a norm for the interpretation of certain rescripts, namely, those that were issued to further the observance of the law. In fact, they insist upon recourse to the law as a means of resolving doubts in rescripts of this nature. The same doctrine is found among the later pre-Code canonists such as Reiffenstuel.[32]

A rescript that is given to further the observance of the law must, as a natural consequence, be interpreted according to the law. A rescript issued by the Holy See to promote the observance of the common law must be understood according to that law. In interpreting such a rescript the previous general authentic interpretations which may have been issued concerning the law, or laws, to which the rescript has reference must also be kept in mind.[33] The same principle applies in the interpretation of a rescript that is issued in accord with some particular law. Thus, Papal rescripts that concern particular legislation of the Holy See must be interpreted in accord with that legislation. A rescript issued by a local Ordinary in a matter determined by diocesan statute should be understood according to the statute, whenever there is any doubt as to its meaning.

Section 5. Circumstances

Various circumstances which attend the issuance of a rescript may also serve as a means of interpreting a particular reply.[34] Circumstances, in general, are accessory and extrinsic conditions, facts or events that accompany, occasion or determine the granting of a rescript. A petition for a rescript is occasioned by a given set of circumstances, i.e., certain facts and events which prompt the petitioner to make a request. These same circumstances influence to some extent the mind and will of the superior who

[32] *Jus Canonicum Universum*, lib. I, tit. III, n. 16.

[33] Cf. Schmidt, *The Principles of Authentic Interpretation*, p. 290.

[34] "Praeterea circumstantiae omnes causarum et personarum diligenter attendendae sunt: nam haec omnia conferunt tum ad significationem verborum, tum ad mentem principis intelligendam."—Suarez, *op. cit.*, lib. VIII, c. 28, n. 19.

grants the reply. Just as they are the occasion for the petition, so, too, they may be the occasion for the rescript.

It will not always be easy to determine the circumstances that influence an ecclesiastical superior in the granting of a rescript. In addition to those mentioned in the petition, there may be others that he will take into consideration. The circumstances which influence the legislator in the drafting of a law can often be known from authentic documents and preparatory acts which precede the actual promulgation of the law.[35] There are usually no such documents and acts available for rescripts. However, the rescript itself may contain a summary of facts and events, as well as the reasons, which prompt the superior to issue the reply. When a rescript is issued in the longer form, such a summary will appear in the *pars narrativa,* and the reasons for granting the rescript will be stated in the *pars motiva.* The fact that they are included is an indication that they are the circumstances and the motives that have influenced the superior in formulating his reply.

Caution, of course, must be exercised in using the circumstances as a means of interpretation. It is not enough to consider them *in se,* or as they actually exist. It is important to know how they are evaluated by the superior who grants the rescript. As noted in the previous paragraph, his estimation of the circumstances may be summarized in the introductory portion of the rescript.

Circumstances which follow upon the granting of a rescript may be of more value as an aid to interpretation than those that precede or accompany its issuance. Of particular significance in this regard is the manner in which the provisions of a rescript have been observed over a period of time. Custom can serve as a norm of interpretation for rescripts as well as laws.[36]

In the course of time doubts may arise concerning the meaning of the terms of a rescript which at first seemed clear. Whenever such doubts do develop, it will be necessary to see how the rescript was interpreted in the beginning. The immediate recipients of the rescript will have been in a position to study the mind of the grantor and to weigh all the circumstances incident to the issuance

[35] Cf. Michiels, *op. cit.,* I, 532, 533.

[36] "Inspicimus in obscuris, quod verisimilius est: vel quod plerumque fieri consuevit."—Reg. 45, R. J., in VI.

of the rescript. Therefore, an attempt should be made to find out how the rescript was understood when first received. Although, *per se,* any previous interpretations that may have been given to a rescript by its recipients do not constitute full proof as to the meaning intended in the rescript, nevertheless, it cannot be denied that such interpretations, if available, are of the utmost value and may serve to remove present doubts. Thus, if a rescript granting the privilege of having Mass celebrated in a private oratory has been in existence for some time, and now doubt should arise about the admittance of certain people, sufficient security can be obtained by learning what the original grantee did.[37]

Section 6. Similar Rescripts

Most of the secondary norms suggested so far for the interpretation of a rescript are intrinsic to the rescript itself. Another, but an extrinsic norm, may also be mentioned. Rescripts granted to persons other than the immediate grantee can oftentimes serve as a source of interpretation. In other words, it may be possible at times to interpret one rescript by recourse to others that are similar.[38]

In a given same set of circumstances, an ecclesiastical superior is accustomed to answer requests for information, advice, favors, etc., in the same way. Therefore, if a particular rescript appears to be obscure, a comparison of it with other rescripts whose contents are similar may help to clarify the doubt. It cannot be emphasized too strongly, however, that such a comparison can be a precarious procedure to follow, since even a slight difference in the circumstances can cause the superior to vary the contents of a rescript. Even where the circumstances surrounding a number of rescripts appear to be identical, the superior is not bound to issue the same reply. As a general rule, however, similar circumstances will evoke a similar reply. Nevertheless, prudence dictates that a careful examination of all the rescripts compared be made before similarity can be used as a norm for interpretation.[39]

---

[37] Cf. Roelker, *op. cit.,* p. 78.

[38] Suarez, *loc. cit.;* Roelker, *op. cit.,* p. 79; Michiels, *op. cit.,* II, 428.

[39] Cf. Roelker, *loc. cit.*

CONCLUSION

The six individual norms mentioned and discussed in the course of this chapter are various means that may be used to clarify doubts that may remain after an attempt has been made to understand a rescript according to the proper meaning of its terms. In regard to the interpretation of laws, canon 18 decrees that certain secondary norms must be employed before a law can be declared doubtful. There is no such express legislation in the Code for the interpretation of rescripts. It is to be expected, however, that when the primary norm fails to reveal the clear meaning of a rescript, other norms will be used before one concludes that the terms of a rescript are doubtful. The norms discussed in this chapter are those that are most likely to be of help. They are the ones mentioned by authors both before and after the Code. Hence, according to canon 20 these norms are to be applied before one may conclude that the terminology of a rescript is doubtful.

CHAPTER V

Negative Norms

The negative norms for the interpretation of rescripts as determined by the Code of Canon Law are set down in canons 49 and 67. Canon 49 contains legislation that is applicable to all rescripts. The canon states that rescripts are to be understood according to the proper meaning of the words and the *communem loquendi usum*, and adds, *"nec debent ad casus alios praeter expressos extendi."* Hence, the canon explicitly forbids the extension of rescripts to cases other than those expressed. Canon 67 contains provisions for the interpretation of privileges. By reason of canon 62, they are applicable to rescripts that grant privileges.[1] In canon 67 the legislator demands that a privilege be understood according to its tenor, and adds, *"nec licet illud extendere aut restringere."* In addition to the prohibition regarding extension, this canon also forbids the restriction of a rescript containing a privilege. In general, then, according to the legislation of the Code, there are two negative norms which govern the interpretation of rescripts. The first concerns the extension of rescripts to other cases; the second concerns the restriction of rescripts which grant privileges. As will be seen in the course of this chapter, the second norm is also valid as a general rule for the interpretation of all rescripts.

ARTICLE I. THE EXTENSION OF RESCRIPTS

The question of the extension of rescripts can become an involved and somewhat difficult one. Much of the difficulty can be obviated by keeping in mind several fundamental principles. First and foremost to be remembered is the principle referred to as the

[1] In Canon 62 the legislator lays down the rule that if a rescript contains not a simple favor, but a privilege or a dispensation, then the prescriptions of the canons pertaining to privileges and dispensations must also be followed. Hence, in addition to the general norms for the interpretation of rescripts, the norms for the interpretation of privileges must be kept in mind.

primary norm for interpretation. The norm directs that rescripts are to be understood according to the proper meaning of their terms. A second principle to be kept in mind contains an exception to the primary norm. According to this second principle, one may never depart from the proper meaning of the words of a rescript, unless it is clear in the text of the rescript that the author of the rescript intends otherwise. To restate the principle in a positive manner, one may depart from the proper meaning of the terms of a rescript, whenever it is certain in the text of the rescript that the author of the rescript clearly intends a meaning other than the proper signification. Both of these principles have been discussed in a previous chapter.[2] They will be referred to again in the course of the present chapter, for the solution to the question of the extension of rescripts depends, to a great extent, upon the correct application of these two important principles.

In addition to these two principles, some idea of the notion and nature of extensive interpretation should be borne in mind. In general, authors agree as to the fundamental notion of this type of interpretation. Extensive interpretation increases the number of persons, cases or things that are to be included within the scope of a law, a rescript or similar legal document. They do not agree, however, as to the *terminus a quo,* or the point of departure whence extensive interpretation proceeds. For the most part, pre-Code authors after the time of Reiffenstuel and canonists after the Code in general, tend to divide themselves into two groups on the question of the *terminus a quo* of extensive interpretation. They consider this question mainly in connection with the interpretation of law. For one group, the *terminus a quo* is the proper meaning of the words. For the other group, it is the mind or intention of the legislator. Thus, for the authors of the first group, interpretation will be extensive when it goes beyond the proper meaning of the words and thereby increases the number of persons, cases, or things that would ordinarily be included within the scope of the law, i.e., within the proper signification of the terms. For those of the second group, interpretation will be extensive when it proceeds beyond the mind of the legislator and thereby increases the number

[2] Cf. *supra,* pp. 51-64.

of persons, cases, or things that would ordinarily be included within the true meaning of the words, i.e., the meaning intended by the legislator, whether that meaning be the proper signification of the terms or some other meaning.[3]

Although the problem of the *terminus a quo* of extensive interpretation has some bearing on the question of the extension of rescripts, for the purposes of the present chapter it will not be necessary to attempt to solve what appears to be an endless controversy. In view of the legislation of the Code regarding the extension of rescripts, the law as it existed before the Code, and the teaching of approved pre-Code canonists, this writer is of the opinion that Suarez' theory of extensive interpretation is best suited to explain the doctrine on extension of rescripts and solve a number of difficulties that arise in connection with the question of the extension of rescripts. For Suarez, the proper meaning of the words is the *terminus a quo,* or point of departure from which extensive interpretation will originate. Regarding extension that goes beyond the proper meaning of words, he makes mention of two types of interpretation, namely, interpretation that extends the proper meaning of words to an improper sense, and interpretation that goes beyond even the improper meaning of words because of the similarity, or identity of the *ratio legis.*[4] In his discussion of the problem of the extension of law beyond the proper meaning of the words by reason of the similarity or identity of the *ratio legis,* Suarez distinguishes between extension that is comprehensive and interpretation which he calls purely extensive. According to him, comprehensive interpretation amounts to an extension of the scope of a law to include a case or person which, while actually an object of the legislator's will, is not well enough expressed in the words of the law.[5] Interpretation that is purely extensive is had when the

[3] It will not be necessary at this time to note the various authors and the opinions which they hold regarding the extensive interpretation of law. It was with this idea in mind that the writer included in Chapter I an article on extensive and restrictive interpretation, in which mention was also made of interpretation that is called comprehensive. The above remarks are but a partial summary of what is contained in that article. Cf. *supra,* pp. 15-24.

[4] *De Legibus,* lib. VI, c. II, n. 2; cf. *supra,* p. 16.

[5] "Comprehensiva interpretatio, vel extensio, est quando per illam declaratur talem casum vel personam comprehensam fuisse in mente legislatoris, licet verbis non satis iam declaraverit. . . ."—*op. cit.,* lib. VI, c. III, n. 9.

disposition of a law is extended, *propter similitudinem vel paritatem rationis,* to include a case not actually the object of the will of the legislator.[6]

In effect, then, Suarez defines comprehensive interpretation as that which goes beyond the words of a law but not beyond the mind of the legislator; purely extensive interpretation as that which goes beyond the words of a law and the mind of the legislator, solely because of the similarity of the *ratio legis.* These two definitions of Suarez, coupled with the two principles mentioned in the beginning of this article, will form the basis for the explanation of the doctrine of the extension of rescripts that now follows.

Before actually beginning that explanation, it should be noted that the legislator of the Code makes no attempt to settle the controversy regarding various species of interpretation and the terminology applicable thereto.[7] In canon 49 he simply directs that rescripts are to be understood according to the proper meaning of their terms and are not to be extended to cases other than those expressed. Canon 67 on privileges contains a similar prohibition in more general terms. In that canon the legislator lays down the rule that a privilege must be understood from its tenor and must not be extended or restricted.

Section 1. Rescripts Are Not to Be Extended to Persons, Cases and Things Not Expressed in the Proper Meaning of the Words

A. The Rule in the Code

The wording of the texts of canon 49 and 67 indicate that, as a general rule at least, rescripts are not to be extended beyond the proper meaning of the words. The first part of canon 49 contains the primary norm for the interpretation of rescripts, which ordains that rescripts are to be understood according to the proper mean-

[6] "Pure vero extensiva mens seu interpretatio dicitur illa per quam extenditur dispositio legis ad casum non comprehensum sub mente legislatoris propter similitudinem vel paritatem rationis."—*loc. cit.*

[7] "Canones 49 et 50 non agunt de interpretatione comprehensiva, restrictiva et extensiva sicut nec canones qui de interpretatione legis agunt. De hac terminologia neque antiqui neque hodierni consentiunt."—Van Hove, *De Rescriptis,* p. 208, note n. 3.

ing of the words and the *communem loquendi usum.* The second part contains a negative norm which states that rescripts are not to be extended to cases other than those expressed. Although the canon contains two norms, a primary and a negative one, the very wording of the canon suggests that the two norms should be understood in conjunction with one another. Indeed, the second part of the canon cannot be understood without reference to the first section. It is not altogether clear from the second section of the canon that rescripts are not to be extended beyond the proper meaning of the words. However, this seems to be the meaning intended in view of the fact that in the preceding section of the canon the legislator demands that rescripts be understood according to the proper meaning of their terms. He follows immediately with the prohibition forbidding their extension to cases not expressed. The conclusion that seems most logical is that rescripts are not to be extended to cases other than those expressed in the proper meaning of the words.

The same conclusion can be drawn from the text of canon 67 which, along with canon 49, is applicable to rescripts in virtue of canon 62. The first part of canon 67 contains a brief and concise version of the primary norm which states simply that a privilege is to be understood according to its tenor, i.e., according to the proper meaning of its words.[8] The second part of the canon forbids not only the extension, but also the restriction of a privilege. Therefore, one should not go beyond or depart from the proper meaning of the terms so as to extend or restrict a privilege.

From the survey of the law prior to the Code that now follows, it will be seen that the foregoing conclusions drawn from canons 49 and 67 are correct. As a general rule, rescripts, including those that grant privileges, are not to be extended so as to include persons, cases and things not expressed in the proper meaning of the terms.

B. The Rule in Decretal Law

It is apparent from the law in the *Corpus Iuris Canonici* that rescripts are not to be understood in such a way as to include

---

[8] Cf. *supra,* pp. 52-54.

persons not mentioned in the rescript. This conclusion is readily deducible from the principle of law enunciated by Pope Alexander III in a letter in which he warns that it is imprudent and improper for one to presume, on his own authority, that what the Church grants to one person for a certain reason, she wishes to bestow on others.[9] In the gloss to this law, the glossator notes that a privilege is not to be extended to persons not expressed in it.[10] The reason for this prohibition, he adds, is that what is granted by means of a privilege ought not to be considered by others, on their own authority, as an example.[11] In support of his statement, he cites a law from the Digest which, when read, shows clearly that the principle laid down by Alexander III has its source in Roman Law. The law states:

> Plane ex his (constitutionibus Imperatorum) quaedam sunt personales nec ad exemplum trahuntur: nam quae princeps alicui ob merita indulsit vel si quam poenam irrogavit vel si cui sine exemplo subvenit, personam non egreditur.[12]

The same principle is repeated elsewhere in the *Corpus Iuris Canonici,* mainly in connection with the interpretation of privileges. It is summarized in the Rule of Law which states: *"Quod alicui gratiose conceditur, trahi non debet ab aliis in exemplum."*[13] A partial list of the Decretals in which the principle is set forth is given in the footnote to canon 67 of the Code.[14] It will not be

---

[9] "Temerarium est et indignum, aliquem sibi sua auctoritate praesumere, quod Romana ecclesia alicui, certa ratione inspecta, singularibus voluit beneficiis indulgere."—C. 9, X, *de privilegiis et excessibus privilegiatorum,* V, 33; Jaffé, n. 4205.

[10] *Glossa ordinaria,* s.v. *Sane.*

[11] *Ibid.,* s.v. *Temerarium.*

[12] D. (1.4) 1, 2. O'Neill points out in his study that many modern authors do not hesitate to classify the *Personales Constitutiones* referred to in the above quotation as rescripts of favor.—*Papal Rescripts of Favor,* p. 8.

[13] Reg. 74, R. J., in VI.

[14] Other Decretals not listed in the footnote to this Canon are mentioned and discussed in an article by Roelker that is worth consulting. Cf. "Additional Sources in the Decretals for the Interpretation of the Law on Privileges," *The Jurist* (Washington, D. C., 1940-), VII (1947), 355-377.

necessary, nor would it be feasible to examine all of these sources. The principle as far as privileges are concerned is clearly evident in the letter of Pope Alexander III quoted in the previous paragraph. It would be well, however, to mention several Decretals which contain the principle as applied to rescripts of justice.

Canon 49 forbids the extension of rescripts to cases that are not expressed in the text of the rescript. One may wonder why no similar prohibition is stated in regard to extension that increases the number of persons that are to be included in a rescript. The main reason would seem to be that the vast majority of the Decretals in the *Corpus Iuris Canonici,* in which the problem of the extension of rescripts in relation to persons is treated, have to do with rescripts of favor, and in particular rescripts in which privileges are granted. The problem does not seem to have presented itself to any great degree in connection with rescripts of justice. This is understandable in view of the fact that a favor that is granted to one person is often desired by others. Extension to persons not mentioned in a rescript is more likely to occur in rescripts of favor than in rescripts of justice, which are concerned mainly with doubts of law and judicial matters. Therefore, the sources containing the principle which forbids the extension of rescripts to persons other than those expressed are cited in the footnote to canon 67 rather than canon 49.

The same principle, however, applies to rescripts in general, as is evident from a letter of Pope Gregory IX (1227-1241) in which he forbids the extension of delegated jurisdiction to persons not expressed in the rescript containing the delegation.[15] In another letter the same Pontiff reprimanded the unwarranted extension of a rescript of justice to a person not mentioned in the rescript.[16] In the very beginning of his commentary on this letter, Panormit-

[15] ". . . iurisdictio delegata ad alias personas quam quae in rescripto continentur prorogari non potest."—C. 40, X, *de officio et potestate judicis delegati,* I, 29, s.v. *Casus.*

[16] C. 34, X, *de rescriptis,* I, 3. The summary to this letter, as given in the *Corpus Iuris Canonici* reads: "Per rescriptum impetratum contra hominem alicuius dioecesis, non extenditur ad hominem eiusdem nominis alterius diocesis."

anus notes that a rescript is to be extended only to the person expressed in it.[17]

The law forbidding the extension of rescripts to cases not expressed is clearly stated in the Decretals. In a letter to the Bishop of Amiens already referred to in a previous article, Pope Alexander III stated that he wished the Knights of the Temple and the Knights Hospitallers to observe the tenor (words) of their privileges, so that they would not exceed their limits.[18] In summarizing the case involved, the glossator to this particular decretal notes that one ought not to exceed the limits of a privilege, and adds that this is an argument proving that the limits of a mandate are to be carefully observed.[19] The last phrase used by the glossator is almost a verbatim repetition of the one used by Boniface VIII (1294-1303) in a letter which reads in part:

> A person appointed by mandate to a non-sacerdotal prebend may not be given, in virtue of the aforesaid mandate, a sacerdotal prebend even with his consent. Similarly, if a mandate enjoins the conferring of a prebend in a church where there are prebends and semi-prebends, a semi-prebend may not be conferred on the recipient of the rescript, even though he may be satisfied with a semi-prebend. So, too, when a mandate orders that one be given a prebend of a certain importance, it may not be executed so as to confer a prebend of less importance, even with that person's consent. For these mandates, whose terms must be carefully observed, ought not to be extended to cases other than those expressed.[20]

The last sentence quoted from the letter is of special importance in regard to the present discussion. In this one compact sentence, Boniface sets forth two principles which govern the extension of rescripts. First of all, the terms of a rescript (mandate) are to be carefully observed. In other words, they are to be understood according to their proper meaning. Boniface does not say this in so many words, but the inference seems warranted in view of what

---

[17] *Commentarium*, lib. I, tit. III, n. 1.

[18] C. 7, X, *de privilegiis et excessibus privilegiatorum*, V, 33.

[19] *Glossa ordinaria*, s.v. *Casus*.

[20] C. 27, *de praebendis et dignitatibus*, III, 4 in VI.

has been said in Chapter III regarding the primary norm for the interpretation of rescripts.[21] Secondly, they are not to be extended to cases other than those expressed. This second principle proposed by Boniface is quoted almost verbatim in canon 49.[22] From the manner in which the Pontiff combines the two principles, a very logical conclusion would seem to be, that rescripts are not to be extended so as to include cases not expressed within the meaning of the terms. This is the same general conclusion that can be drawn from the same two principles as stated in canon 49.

Section 2. The Reasons for the Rule

There are several reasons for the rule prohibiting the extension of rescripts to persons and cases not expressed. For one thing, the very nature of a rescript suggests the rule. A rescript is an answer to a particular inquiry. The inquiry, or petition, is the cause, or the occasion, of the rescript, and hence, the reply is formulated in view of the peculiar circumstances, conditions and persons mentioned in the request. The rescript is the means used by the ecclesiastical superior to make known his intention in regard to these circumstances, conditions and persons.[23] The value of a rescript, then, depends ultimately upon the will or intention of the one who issues it. In granting such a reply, the superior intends that the provisions of the rescript be limited to certain persons and cases. This is the main reason why a rescript should not be extended to other persons and cases.

Reiffenstuel supports this conclusion clearly in regard to priv-

---

[21] In that chapter the letter of Alexander III to the Bishop of Amiens, mentioned above, was cited and discussed as a source for the primary norm for the interpretation of rescripts. In the letter, Alexander declared that he wished the Knights of the Temple and the Knights Hospitallers to observe the tenor of their privileges, i.e., to understand them according to the proper meaning of their terms. Boniface uses almost the same words in his letter. Cf. *supra*, pp. 52-54.

[22] The principle as stated by Pope Boniface reads: "Non enim huiusmodi mandata (quorum fines diligenter servari opòrtet) debent ad casus alios quam expressos extendi." Canon 49 states: "Rescripta . . . nec debent ad casus alios praeter expressos extendi."

[23] Concerning the notion and nature of a rescript, cf. *supra*, pp. 32-35.

ileges and other favors in his commentary on Rule 74 of the *Regulae Juris.*[24] The reason for the rule, according to him, is that favors and privileges (*gratiae speciales contra jus*) derive their value from the intention and will of the one who grants them. The intention of the grantor, however, is not that such favors and privileges be extended to others besides the grantee, *"sed tanquam favor, et privilegium personale personam duntaxat sequatur, et cum ea extinguatur."* Therefore, they should not be considered by others as an example to be followed.[25]

The same rule applies to rescripts in general, for all rescripts are to be considered as favors, in the sense that the ecclesiastical superior who grants even a rescript of justice is not obliged to do so.[26] What the author of a rescript freely grants or states in a particular reply, he does not intend as an example to be followed by others.

Moreover, what the author of a rescript intends in a given reply, he makes known by means of the words which he uses. One should not depart from the meaning of the words, unless it is clear that the author of the rescript intends otherwise.[27] This principle offers a second very cogent reason for not extending rescripts. To extend the terms of a rescript to cases and persons not expressed in them is to depart from the meaning of the terms. Therefore, as a general rule rescripts should not be extended to persons and cases not expressed in the terms of the rescript. This is the reasoning followed by Schmalzgrueber in his discussion of the extension of privileges.[28] Ojetti applies the same reasoning to the question of the extension of rescripts.[29]

---

[24] "Quod alicui gratiose conceditur, trahi non debet ab aliis in exemplum."

[25] *Tractatus de Regulis Juris* (Romae, 1834), Reg. 74, n. 3.

[26] "Gratia conceditur etiam in rescriptis ad lites."—Van Hove, *De Rescriptis,* n. 88; cf. also Panormitanus, *Commentarium,* lib. V, tit. 40, c. 16, n. 7.

[27] Cf. *supra,* pp. 51, 52.

[28] According to him, extension in the interpretation of privileges is usually not allowed, and he gives as the first reason the following: "Ratio est 1. quia efficacia privilegii pendet ex intentione concedentis, quae intentio significatur verbis; ergo ultra expressionem verborum non debet fieri extensio et hinc est, quod communiter dicitur, *privilegia valere tantum quantum sonant";—Jus Ecclesiasticum Universum,* lib. V, tit. 33, n. 139.

[29] *Commentarium,* I, 246.

Section 3. The Effects of the Rule

A. In Regard to Extension by Analogy of Subject Matter

From the foregoing consideration of the reasons for the rule prohibiting the extension of rescripts, it follows that a rescript may not be extended to other persons and cases merely because there is a similarity between them and the person or cases mentioned in the rescript. Thus, interpretation by way of analogy is forbidden.[30] Although such interpretation is allowed with respect to laws,[31] it has no place in the interpretation of rescripts. It matters little that the conditions, circumstances, etc., which occasion a rescript are verified in regard to other persons or cases. The rescript may not be understood to include either the persons or the cases. The main reason, of course, is that the will or intention of the one who issues the rescript is concerned only with the persons or cases mentioned in the reply. Unlike a law, a rescript is not a general norm intended for widespread application. I'ts scope is limited to particular persons, cases or things.

B. In Regard to Extension *ob Similitudinem vel Identitatem Rationis*

A rescript may not be extended to other persons, cases or things even when there is an equal or greater reason for their inclusion within the terms of the rescript than for those that are actually included and contained therein.[32] The reason for this rule, as already indicated in the previous section, is that the value and force of a rescript depends ultimately upon the will or intention of its author and not upon the reason for which it is granted.[33]

In his treatise on privileges, Suarez mentions the fact that in the *Corpus Iuris Canonici* there appears to be contradictory legisla-

---

[30] Cf. Michiels, *Normae Generales,* II, 424; O'Neill, *op. cit.,* pp. 101, 102; Van Hove, *De Rescriptis,* n. 222.

[31] Cf. can. 18 and its reference to parallel places.

[32] Cf. O'Neill, *loc. cit.*

[33] "Etenim vis rescripti non est essentialiter in ratione ob quam datur, sed in voluntate concedentis quae non extenditur ob identitatem rationis."—Van Hove, *loc. cit.*

tion regarding their interpretation.[34] Some decretals, he notes, call for their restriction,[35] while others direct that they be extended.[36] During the course of his discussion, he solves this apparent contradiction by showing that although some privileges are to be interpreted broadly, they may never be interpreted extensively, i.e., by pure extension.[37] According to Suarez' definition, interpretation that is purely extensive is had when the disposition of a law is extended, because of a similarity of the *ratio* or purpose of the law, to a case not actually the object of the will of the legislator.[38] In his treatise on the interpretation of law, he concludes that such interpretation goes beyond the mind of the legislator, and therefore, is reserved to the legislator alone.[39] In treating of the interpretation of privileges by those other than the authentic interpreter, he reaches a similar conclusion. A privilege may never be extended to other persons or cases *propter similitudinem rationis.* The reason for this, according to him, is that the efficacy of a privilege depends upon the will of its author and not upon the reason for which it is granted. Therefore, he adds, it matters little that in a similar case or in regard to a similar person the same reason exists, as long as the will of the grantor does not extend to them.[40]

The same line of reasoning can be followed in regard to the interpretation of rescripts.[41] The principles are the same. Extension because of a similarity, or even the identity, of the *ratio* or purpose for which a rescript is granted is not allowed in rescripts for the very same reason that extension in general is forbidden. The power and efficacy of a rescript depends upon the will or intention of the ecclesiastical superior who issues it. The number of persons, cases

---

[34] *De Legibus,* lib. VIII, c. 27, n. 1.

[35] C. 7, 9, X, *de privilegiis et excessibus privilegiatorm,* V, 33.

[36] C. 16, X, *de verborum significatione,* V, 40.

[37] *Op. cit.,* lib. VIII, c. 28, n. 3; cf. White, *The Evolution of the Canonical Concept of Strict Interpretation of Law,* pp. 22, 23.

[38] *Op. cit.,* lib. VI, c. III, n. 9.

[39] *Ibid.,* n. 10.

[40] *Op. cit.,* lib. VIII, c. 28, n. 11; cf. also Schmalzgrueber, *op. cit.,* lib. V, tit. 33, n. 143; Grandclaude, *Jus Canonicum,* lib. V, Sectio III, n. 2.

[41] Cf. Van Hove, *De Rescriptis,* n. 222.

or things that are to be included within the terms of a particular rescript is not governed by the *ratio rescripti* or the reason why it is issued. It rests wholly upon the will of the superior.

The problem, then, is to determine the extent of the mind or intention of the superior, i.e., the number of persons, cases, etc., that he intends to include within the content of a rescript. As Suarez points out in regard to privileges, the meaning of the words reveals how far the will of the grantor extends.[42] Suarez' solution to the problem is substantially the same as the one that has already been given in Sections 1 and 2 of this chapter. As a general rule, rescripts are not to be understood in such a way as to include persons, cases or things that are not expressed in the proper meaning of the terms. From what has been said in this section, it can be seen that no exception is to be made to this rule in order to allow extension by analogy of person or object, or because of a similarity or identity of the *ratio* or purpose for which a rescript is issued. There is, however, one main exception to this rule which will now be discussed in the following section.

Section 4. The Exception to the Rule

As pointed out in Chapter III, one may never depart from the proper meaning of the terms of a rescript unless it is clear that the author of the rescript intends otherwise.[43] Where the author of a rescript clearly intends otherwise, one not only may but must depart, to some extent, from the proper meaning of the words. Since the purpose of interpretation in regard to rescripts is to discover the mind or intention of the superior who grants the rescript, some departure from the proper meaning of the words will be necessary whenever it is clear that what the author intends is other than the proper meaning of the terms would seem to indicate. In other words, the proper meaning of the terms should

---

[42] "Non autem extenditur si non exprimitur, quia (ut saepe dixi) inter homines voluntas non operatur, nisi ut significata."—*loc. cit.*

[43] Cf. *supra*, 52-54. "Ut a proprio sensu verborum recedatur, invicte probandum est aliam esse mentem rescribentis."—Van Hove, *De Rescriptis*, n. 221.

not be preferred to the mind or intention of the author, whenever the latter is clearly known.[44]

This is the meaning of the principle enunciated in a canon of the Decree of Gratian which states: "non debet aliquis verba considerare, sed voluntatem et intentionem, quia non debet intentio verbis deservire, sed verba intentioni.[45] In his commentary on this canon, Gratian reduces the text to an axiom: *"Intentio non debet deservire verbis, sed verba intentioni."* The principle in no way weakens the value of the primary norm of interpretation. Ordinarily, words are used according to their proper meaning and the *communem loquendi usum* and, therefore, should be understood in that sense. At times, however, it will be manifest that a meaning other than the proper signification is intended. If the meaning intended is clearly apparent, then the words should be understood according to the mind or intention of their author and not according to their proper meaning.[46]

Where it is evident that the author of a rescript intends that persons and cases other than those expressed in the proper meaning of the words be included within the scope of a rescript, then the rescript must be understood according to the mind or intention of the author. This is the conclusion reached by Pirhing in his treatise on the interpretation of rescripts. When discussing the question of the extension of a rescript to a case not expressed, he notes that such extension is forbidden unless it is clear that the author of the rescript intends otherwise. If such is the case, he adds, then one must depart from the proper and commonly accepted meaning of the words, because the intention of the author

---

[44] "Si quaeritur de interpretatione rescriptorum vel privilegiorum; tunc magis stadum est intentione scribentis si de ipsa appareat quam verbis scripturae."—Hostiensis, *Summa Aurea,* lib. V, *De verborum significatione,* n. 6.

[45] C. 11, C. 22, q. 5—*Decretum Gratiani emendatum et notationibus illustratum una cum glossis* (2 vols., Romae, 1582).

[46] "Imprimis verba ordinarie sunt exaudienda secundum propriam significationem vel communem loquendi usum maxime dum ratio urgens non obstat: . . . Si mens et intentio loquentis alias appareat verba ad eum sensum sunt explicanda . . . quia verba pendent a mente non autem mens a verbis"; —Böckhn, *Commentarium,* lib. V, tit. XL, nn. 1, 2.

is to be preferred to the meaning of the words, whenever the intention can be known for certain. The ultimate reason for this departure, he notes, is that words are used to signify the mind or intention of a speaker or writer, and hence, *"si de illa constet, non est habenda ratio verborum."*[47]

There seems to be some question as to whether the only exception to the general rule forbidding the extension of rescripts to persons and cases not expressed is the one noted above, namely, when it is clear that the author of a rescript intends that persons and cases other than those expressed in the proper meaning of the words be included within the scope of the rescript. From what has been said up to this point, it would seem that there is no other exception. However, a number of pre-Code authors, notably Suarez,[48] Pirhing,[49] Reiffenstuel,[50] Schmalzgrueber,[51] and Grandclaude,[52] in their treatises on the interpretation of privileges mention several different occasions when it would be permissible, and even necessary at times, to understand a privilege in such a way as to include persons and cases that are not actually contained in the proper meaning of the words. What they have to say concerns privileges in general and is therefore applicable to rescripts that grant privileges.

It will not be necessary to consider each of these authors individually, for their theories are in substantial agreement. The main problem that confronts them is the question of the extension of privileges. In attempting to solve the question, they distinguish between interpretation that is truly extensive and interpretation that includes persons and cases that are virtually contained within the proper meaning of the terms of a privilege. True extension, or interpretation that goes beyond the mind of the author of a privilege, they do not allow. They do permit, however, favorable privileges to be interpreted in such a way as to include persons

---

[47] *Jus Canonicum,* lib. I, tit. III, n. 28.
[48] *Op. cit.,* lib. VIII, c. 28, nn. 11-14.
[49] *Op. cit.,* lib. V, tit. XXXIII, nn. 21-25.
[50] *Op. cit.,* lib. V, tit. XXXIII, nn. 95-100.
[51] *Op. cit.,* lib. V, tit. XXXIII, nn. 131-140.
[52] *Op. cit.,* lib. V, sec. III, n. 2.

and cases that are at least virtually contained within the terms of this type of privilege.[53]

Suarez describes such interpretation as extension *"per virtualem continentiam veroborum, juxta rationabilem eorum interpretationem."* While he does not actually use the expression *"interpretatio comprehensiva,"* it is evident from what he has to say in general about the interpretation of privileges, that he has this form of interpretation in mind when he speaks of extension *per virtualem continentiam verborum*. Such extension, according to him, *"plura comprehendat quam superficie verborum appareat."*[54] Grandclaude describes it as interpretation that makes known a case or person which, while not expressed in a privilege, is virtually and implicitly contained therein and is within the mind of the legislator. Such interpretation is permitted, according to him, because it is not true extension (which goes beyond the mind of the author), but interpretation that is comprehensive (which stays within the mind of the author).[55]

To summarize briefly, it can be said that all of the pre-Code authors mentioned above contend that privileges are not to be interpreted in such a way as to include persons and cases not expressed within the proper meaning of the terms. They base their conclusion on the fact that the mind or intention of the author of a privilege is known, as a general rule, only through the proper meaning of the terms which he uses. They agree, however, that there are certain times when additional persons and cases are to be looked upon as being virtually contained within the scope of a privilege although they are not actually and formally contained within the proper meaning of its terms. They consider the inclusion of these additional persons and cases to be a form of extension which, since it does not go beyond the mind or intention of the

---

[53] They do not allow odious privileges to be interpreted in this manner for the reason that they are to be restricted.

[54] *Op. cit.*, lib. VIII, c. 28, n. 14. Suarez defines comprehensive interpretation in his treatise on law as that form of interpretation which broadens the scope of a law to include a person or case which, while actually an object of the legislator's will, is not well enough expressed in the words of the law. —*op. cit.*, lib. VI, c. 2, n. 9.

[55] *Loc. cit.;* cf. also Schmalzgrueber, *op. cit.*, lib. V, tit. XXXIII, n. 131.

author of the privilege, is permissible, and even necessary at times, in virtue of one or another of a variety of reasons or causes, e.g., the subject matter of the privilege, custom, the law, or because the author clearly intends that they be included. Thus, the subject matter of a privilege may be of such a nature that, unless some person or persons other than the immediate grantee are included, the privilege would be useless or unjust. Similarly, the law itself may demand that a privilege be understood as including a person or case not actually mentioned in the privilege, e.g., the privilege of saying Mass in time of interdict would include the right of the server to assist at the Mass, since the law requires the celebrant to have a server.[56]

Among modern authors, Van Hove, in his discussion of the interpretation of rescripts, repeats in substance the doctrine of the pre-Code authors outlined above. In regard to the extension of rescripts he makes specific mention of the fact that a rescript may be extended *"ad omnia quae virtualiter in verbis comprehenduntur."* Further on in the same number in which he treats the extension of rescripts, he points out several ways in which a rescript granting a privilege may be understood so as to include a person or thing that is not actually mentioned in the privilege.[57]

According to Regatillo, a privilege may be extended to a person or case other than those expressed in order that the privilege may not be useless. He refers to this form of interpretation as *extensio logica.*[58] According to Roelker, comprehensive interpretation is admissible in privileges. Such an interpretation, he states, conforms to the mind of the legislator rather than to his words. He gives several examples by way of illustration, but gives no reason why such interpretation is admissible other than the fact that it conforms to the mind of the legislator.[59]

---

[56] Cf. Schmalzgrueber, *ibid.,* nn. 136, 137, 140.

[57] "Subjectum privilegii est tantum persona vel res cui actu conceditur privilegium et quae in ipso privilegio exprimitur, vel quae ex vi vocis aut actionis seu materiae aut ex aliqua iuris dispositone sub illa comprehenditur." —*De Rescriptis,* n. 222.

[58] *Institutiones,* I, 105.

[59] "Thus, by means of comprehensive interpretation, a privilege conceded to a hospital includes those who work there, or, a privilege to say mass during an interdict includes the server, etc."—*Principles of Privilege,* p. 71.

From what was said in the first few paragraphs of this section, it should be apparent that the extension of rescripts (including rescripts which grant privileges) to persons and cases not expressed is permissible only when it is clear that the author of the rescript intends that such an interpretation be given. This idea is what Roelker seems to have in mind when he states that comprehensive interpretation is admissible in privileges since it conforms to the mind of the legislator. It would also seem that the same idea is uppermost in the minds of the pre-Code canonists, mentioned above, in their discussions of the interpretation of privileges.

Although these authors mention the subject matter of a privilege, custom, the law and various other juridic factors in virtue of which comprehensive interpretation is permissible, or necessary, in a privilege, the ultimate reason for such an interpretation would seem to be found in the mind or intention of the author of the privilege. The authors cited do not neglect to mention the intention of the author as a reason for the inclusion of additional persons and cases within the proper meaning of the terms of a privilege. However, they do not specifically mention the fact that the intention of the author, as verified by these means, is the ultimate reason why such extension is permitted or demanded. This conclusion is implied, it seems, in their assertions that extension *per virtualem continentiam* is not forbidden in view of the fact that it is not true extension, i.e, it does not go beyond the mind of the author of a privilege.

While the subject matter of a privilege, custom, the law, etc., may be considered as reasons in virtue of which persons and cases other than those actually expressed within the proper meaning of the terms of a privilege may be included within the scope of the privilege, they may also be looked upon as various means which may be used to show that the mind or intention of the author of a privilege (or rescript) is other than the mere proper meaning of the words would seem to indicate. In other words, they may be considered as means of interpretation. They serve to make known what the author of a privilege (or rescript) intends over and above what is actually expressed in the words that he uses. Thus, from the law which requires the celebrant of Mass to have a server,[60] one may conclude that the author of a privilege, which allows a priest to celebrate Mass during an interdict, intends also that the privilege be understood in such a way as to allow the server to assist at the Mass, even though no mention is made of the server in the text of the privilege. A similar conclusion follows from the law which directs that the grantee of a privilege derive some benefit from the good will of the grantor.[61] When a privilege would be useless unless a person other than the immediate grantee were included, one may conclude that the author intends that the privilege be extended to include that other person.

It may seem that undue emphasis is being placed on the use of the subject matter of a privilege, the law, custom, and other juridic factors, such as rules of law, as norms of interpretation rather than as reasons which, in themselves, allow the extension of a privilege (or rescript) to persons and cases not actually expressed. By considering them as means of interpretation, it can be seen more clearly that there is only one exception to the rule which forbids the extension or rescripts to persons and cases not expressed in the proper meaning of the terms. Namely, only where it is evident that the author of a rescript intends otherwise, may one depart from the proper meaning of its terms, so as to include persons and cases not actually mentioned. These means may make it evident that a departure is intended; they are the principles and, hence, the reasons of such departure.

This is the conclusion arrived at earlier in Chapter III and repeated in the very beginning of this section. It is the conclusion reached by Pirhing in his treatise on the interpretation of rescripts. What Pirhing himself and the other pre-Code authors cited above have to say in regard to the interpretation of privileges tends to support, rather than weaken, this position. The principle contained in the conclusion is the one that ultimately governs all departures from the norm forbidding the extension of rescripts.

In applying the principle, it is necessary to determine when the mind or intention of the author of a rescript is other than the proper meaning of the words seems to indicate. There must be

---

[60] Cf. can. 813, § 1.

[61] Cf. can. 68.

some clear and definite indication that the author of a rescript intends to include persons and cases not actually expressed in the proper meaning of its terms before an interpretation that goes beyond the proper meaning of the terms is permissible. One may not conclude that such is the intention of the author unless there is some juridic principle for doing so. Some of the principles, or means, for ascertaining that such is the intention of the author have already been noted. The principal means are the law itself, the subject matter of a rescript, custom, and the *stylus Curiae*. The use of these means is sanctioned by the present law in virtue of canon 20 in general, as well as several prescriptions of the Code in particular. For example, according to canon 200, § 1, it is understood that the person who receives delegated jurisdiction is granted all those powers without which the exercise of his delegated power would be impossible.[62]

ARTICLE II. THE RESTRICTIVE INTERPRETATION OF RESCRIPTS

The restriction of rescripts is governed by the same principles of interpretation that regulate their extension. It will be sufficient, then, in this article to give some idea of the notion of restrictive interpretation and to show how the principles are applicable. It should be noted in the beginning, however, that while canon 49 explicitly forbids the extension of rescripts to cases other than those expressed, it makes no mention of the restriction of rescripts. It does not follow from this seeming omission that restriction in rescripts is not forbidden. Canon 67 explicitly states that it is not permissible to extend or restrict a privilege. By reason of canon 62, understood in conjunction with canon 49, this provision of canon 67 is applicable to rescripts that grant privileges. Therefore, as far as rescripts that contain privileges are concerned, the Code does expressly forbid restriction. As will be seen, the same prohibition against restriction is valid as a general norm for the interpretation of all rescripts.

As the name implies, restrictive interpretation restricts or limits the number of persons, cases, or things that are to be included

---

[62] Cf. also cans. 1051, 1053.

within the scope of a rescript. This writer favors the majority opinion among authors, that the proper meaning of the words of a rescript constitutes the *terminus a quo* or point of departure for restrictive interpretation.[63] To restrict a rescript, then, means to depart from the proper meaning of the terms of a rescript in such a way as to lessen or reduce the number of persons, cases or things that would ordinarily be included within its terminology. Restrictive interpretation must not be confused with strict interpretation. The latter form of interpretation always remains within the proper meaning of words. It merely limits that meaning to its narrowest confines. Restrictive interpretation entails a departure from the proper meaning of words. The departure is such that the words are understood in a narrower or restricted sense than their proper meaning. As the result of a restrictive interpretation, fewer persons, cases or things are comprehended within the scope of a rescript than would be included were the reply understood according to even the narrowest proper meaning of its terms.[64]

As a general rule, restrictive interpretation is forbidden in rescripts. One may not depart from the proper meaning of the terms of a rescript so as to lessen the number of persons, cases or things that are included within the text of the reply. As a negative norm for the interpretation of rescripts, this prohibition against restriction is but a natural and logical consequence of the primary norm of interpretation, which directs that rescripts are to be understood according to the proper meaning of their terms. This is the line of reasoning followed by Pope Boniface VIII in one of his letters, a portion of which was quoted in the previous article.[65] In the letter, Boniface decreed that a mandate ordering a prebend of a certain importance to be given to a person could not be executed so as to confer a prebend of less importance, even with that person's consent. The Pontiff's directive amounts to a prohibition against the restriction of a rescript. Boniface gives the reason for

---

[63] Cf. *supra*, p. 20.
[64] Cf. *supra*, pp. 15-24.
[65] C. 27, *de praebendis et dignitatibus*, III, 4 in VI. Cf. *supra*, p. 86.

the rule when he states that the terms of such a mandate must be carefully observed.[66]

As noted and discussed in the previous article, the only time one may depart from the proper meaning of the terms of a rescript is when there are clear indications of a juridic nature that show that the author of a rescript intends that the text of his reply be given a meaning other than the proper signification.[67] When it is evident that the author of a rescript intends that the terms of his reply be restricted in such a way as to exclude certain persons, cases or things that would otherwise be included within the proper meaning of the terms of the rescript, then the rescript must be understood according to the mind or intention of the author.

There are various means or juridic norms for ascertaining that such is the intention of the author of a rescript. Some of the means have already been mentioned in connection with the discussion of extensive interpretation. Thus, custom, the law itself, or the *stylus Curiae* may indicate that certain persons, cases or things are not to be included within the terms of a particular rescript. Canon 2253, § 3, for example, states that the general faculty to absolve from censures that are reserved to the Apostolic See does not include the power to absolve from censures that are reserved in a special or most special way to the Apostolic See. Hence, the law itself would exclude certain censures from the scope of a rescript granting such a general faculty.[68]

The above provision of canon 2253, § 3 is an application of Rule 81 of the *Regulae Juris* in VI.[69] The rule itself may serve as one of the norms for ascertaining that the author of a rescript intends to exclude certain persons, cases, etc., from the text of a rescript. As applied to rescripts, the rule directs that general terms in a

---

[66] Cf. also c. 4, 13, X, *de privilegiis et excessibus privilegiatorum,* V, 33.

[67] Cf. *supra,* pp. 91, 92.

[68] A similar restriction is found in canon 1403, § 1, which ordains that persons who have obtained from the Holy See the permission to read and keep forbidden books cannot for that reason read and keep books forbidden by their own Ordinaries, unless the Apostolic indult explicitly grants them the faculty to read and keep books forbidden by *any* authority.

[69] "In generali concessione non veniunt ea quae quis non esset verisimiliter in specie concessurus."

rescript should not be understood to include what the author of the rescript would most likely specifically mention in granting a reply, had he intended inclusion. Whenever things that are deserving of special mention are not specifically referred to in a rescript, one should conclude that the author of the rescript purposely omitted them. Therefore, they should be considered as not being included with the terms of the rescript.[70]

While custom, the law, and the *stylus Curiae* may be looked upon as norms indicating that the mind or intention of the author of a rescript is other than the proper meaning of the words would seem to denote, what they actually do is determine the proper meaning of the words. Therefore, any interpretation that restricts the meaning of the terms of a rescript in virtue of these norms is not a restrictive interpretation in the strict sense.[71]

In practice, a restrictive interpretation that departs from the proper meaning of the terms of a rescript will be rare. For one other than the authentic interpreter, it would be permissible only when it is clear that the author of a rescript intends that the text of his reply be restricted even to the point of departing from the proper meaning of the words. Such a departure would obviously be intended when a mere declarative interpretation would presuppose an injustice on the part of the author of a rescript.[72] One should not presume that the author of a rescript intends an injustice in issuing a rescript. However, a rescript should not be considered unjust merely because it grants a favor or contains a provision that is unfavorable or burdensome to a third party. It would be unjust if, because of peculiar circumstances of time, place or person, its use entailed a departure from the divine natural or positive law.[73] The concession of an unusually generous favor or

[70] Reiffenstuel, *Tractatus de Regulis Juris,* Reg. 81, n. 3; Michiels, *Normae Generales,* II, 427; O'Neill, *Papal Rescripts of Favor,* p. 101; Van Hove, *De Rescriptis,* n. 223.

[71] Cf. Van Hove, *loc. cit.*

[72] Suarez, *De Legibus,* lib. VIII, c. 28, nn. 3, 4; Michiels, *op. cit.,* II, 426; O'Neill, *loc. cit.,* Van Hove, *loc. cit.*

[73] "Si iniquitas solum oriatur ex lege positiva dispensabili ab eo, qui privilegium [vel rescriptum in genere] concedit, jam illa non manet concesso privilegio, quia legis obligatio per illud aufertur, et ita in usu talis privilegii per se loquendo nulla est iniquitas."—Suarez, *op. cit.,* lib. VIII, c. 28, n. 5.

relaxation of the law in a rescript might appear to be an injustice on the part of the author of a rescript. One could not presume therefrom that a restrictive interpretation was intended, for there is always the possibility that the superior who grants such a favor has special reasons, unknown to others, which explain his extraordinary generosity.[74]

[74] Suarez, *op. cit.,* lib. VIII, c. 28, n. 8; Michiels, *loc. cit.;* O'Neill, *loc. cit.*

PART III

The Special Norms for the Interpretation of Rescripts

INTRODUCTION

Part II of the present study was devoted to an explanation of the general norms for the interpretation of rescripts. The third and final part that now follows will be concerned with a discussion of the special norms for their interpretation. The special norms for the interpretation of rescripts are to be used only when the primary and secondary general norms have failed to reveal the meaning intended in a rescript. Their chief function is to serve as means for the interpretation of doubtful rescripts. It is for this reason that they are referred to as special norms.

The special norms for the interpretation of rescripts can be reduced to two categories. In the first category are contained all the norms that have to do with the strict interpretation of rescripts. In the second category there is only one norm, which governs the broad interpretation of rescripts. The two chapters that comprise Part III will treat each of these categories separately. Chapter VI will be concerned with rescripts that are subject to strict interpretation. Chapter VII will consider rescripts that are to be given a broad interpretation.

The special norms for the interpretation of rescripts are found principally in canon 50 of the Code of Canon Law. This canon will serve as the point of departure for the majority of the observations and explanations that will be given in the subsequent chapters. Consideration will also be given to canons 68 and 85 in so far as they treat of the interpretation of rescripts that grant privileges and dispensations. These three canons, in particular, contain the present legislation on the strict and broad interpretation of rescripts. In commenting on them, frequent reference will be made to the law as it existed before the Code and to the works of approved pre-Code authors.

CHAPTER VI

The Strict Interpretation of Rescripts

The strict interpretation of rescripts under the present law of the Code is determined primarily by canon 50. The canon gives no definition of strict interpretation, nor does it give any indication as to why the rescripts which it mentions are to be given such an interpretation. According to the canon, in doubt, the following rescripts are to be strictly interpreted: 1) rescripts which refer to litigation; 2) those that are adverse to the acquired rights of others; 3) rescripts which grant to private individuals favors that are against the law, and finally; 4) those which were obtained for the purpose of acquiring an ecclesiastical benefice.[1]

By reason of canon 68, the provisions of canon 50 are applicable also to the interpretation of doubtful privileges. There is one added stipulation in the former canon, however, which must be noted. According to canon 68, a doubtful privilege is always to be interpreted in such a way that the recipients of the privilege derive some benefit from the favor that is granted to them.[2] As canon 62 directs, this special provision of canon 68 must also be observed in the interpretation of rescripts that grant privileges.

Canon 85 contains legislation similar in wording to that which is found in canon 68. It prescribes that dispensations, as well as the faculty granted to dispense in a certain case, are to be strictly interpreted in accordance with canon 50.[3] With the exception of

---

[1] "In dubio, rescripta quae ad lites referuntur, vel iura aliis quaesita laedunt, vel adversantur legi in commodum privatorum, vel denique impetrata fuerunt ad beneficii ecclesiastici assecutionem, strictam interpretationem recipiunt."

[2] "In dubio privilegia interpretanda sunt ad normam can. 50; sed ea semper adhibenda interpretatio, ut privilegio aucti aliquam ex indulgentia concedentis videantur gratiam consecuti."

[3] "Strictae subest interpretationi non solum dispensatio ad normam can. 50, sed ipsamet facultas dispensandi ad certum casum concessa."

its latter clause, canon 85 proposes no norms other than those that are already set forth in canon 50. No special consideration will have to be given to it apart from some discussion of the notions of dispensation and the faculty to dispense in a certain case.

It hardly needs to be noted, that, of the three canons mentioned above, the principal and all important one as far as the strict interpretation of rescripts is concerned is canon 50. It deals only with rescripts. The other two canons require special consideration in so far as they affect privileges, dispensations and the faculty to dispense that are granted by means of a rescript. With the exception of the added proviso concerning the effect of privileges that is indicated in canon 68, and the latter clause of canon 85, they merely repeat the legislation that is contained in canon 50.

ARTICLE I. THE CRITERIA OF A DOUBTFUL RESCRIPT

According to canon 50, the special norms for the interpretation of rescripts are not to be used unless the meaning of a rescript is doubtful. Not any and every doubt that may arise concerning the meaning of the terms of a rescript will warrant the use of these norms. One may have doubts about the meaning of a rescript that, in itself, is clear and understandable. Such doubts will be subjective rather than objective. They may arise for a number of reasons, e.g., through ignorance, inadvertence or the failure to take into consideration some circumstance or detail of a rescript, or principle of law, or of juridic interpretation. They will be in the mind of the interpreter rather than in the text of the rescript. Of themselves, they are not sufficient to render the text of a rescript doubtful according to the meaning of canon 50.

As pointed out in Chapter III, the primary norm of interpretation will usually reveal the meaning intended in a rescript. It is for this reason that the legislator demands, first of all, that rescripts be understood according to the proper meaning of their terms. There are times, however, when the proper meaning of the terms of a rescript will remain doubtful or obscure. As indicated in Chapter IV, when the primary norm fails to achieve its intended result, an attempt must be made to dispel any doubts that remain through the use of the secondary norms of interpretation. The secondary norms for the interpretation of rescripts are limited in number. Only those that are sanctioned by law may be used. Once these norms have been applied, and it is still impossible to determine the meaning intended in a rescript, one may conclude that the text of the rescript is doubtful.[4]

The primary and secondary norms of interpretation are the criteria that determine whether a rescript is clear or doubtful and hence, whether or not canon 50 may be invoked. Once the meaning of a rescript becomes clear through the use of these primary and secondary norms, the need for interpretation ceases. The rescript can be considered as being *in se* clear. The norms will have served to make known what was already objectively contained in the rescript. They will have fulfilled their chief function, which is to manifest the inherent clarity of the text of a rescript.

The fact that the primary and secondary norms of interpretation fail to make known the meaning intended in a rescript is reason enough to conclude that the terminology of the rescript itself is doubtful. The doubt that remains is more than a mere subjective doubt. It will be in the text itself, and not only in the mind of the one who is seeking to interpret the rescript. In other words, it will be an objective doubt. In this writer's opinion, this is the doubt that is envisioned in canon 50. Other than the primary and secondary norms, there are no juridically approved norms for the declarative interpretation of rescripts. The special norms mentioned in canon 50 have to do with the interpretation that may be called explanatory.[5] The very wording of canons 49 and 50 seems to indicate that this conclusion is correct. Further evidence to support this conclusion can be had from a comparative study of canons 49 and 50 with canons 18 and 19, which contain similar legislation for the interpretation of law. According to canon 18, ecclesiastical laws are to be interpreted according to the primary norm, i.e., the proper signification of the terms. If the text of a

---

[4] Cf. in particular the conclusion to Chapter IV, p. 78.

[5] Cf. *supra,* pp. 10-15 for an explanation of declarative and explanatory interpretation.

law remains doubtful and obscure after the application of the primary norm, then the canon directs that certain secondary norms are to be used. If the text of the law still remains doubtful, what then? It would seem, then, that the text itself of the law is objectively doubtful. There must be some objective juridic norm to determine the presence of doubt.

Canon 49 operates in a similar way in regard to rescripts. In a rescript, the objective doubt, if any, is established by the norms of interpretation embodied in canon 49. Canon 50 cannot be invoked unless the text of a rescript remains doubtful after the application of the primary and secondary norms of canon 49. If the meaning of a rescript is still uncertain after their application, then there would seem to be, by positive law, a *dubium* in regard to the text itself. When such a doubt exists, interpretation of a so-called explanatory nature becomes necessary. For those other than the authentic interpreter, the only legally permissible means that may be used in order to clarify the doubt are those that are mentioned in canon 50. If doubt still persists after the terms of a rescript have been either strictly or broadly interpreted, then the only other alternative is to have recourse to the grantor, or his successor, or their delegate for an authentic interpretation of the rescript.[6]

ARTICLE II. STRICT INTERPRETATION

Canon 50 gives no definition nor indication of the notion and nature of strict interpretation. It merely directs that, in doubt, certain types of rescripts are subject to this form of interpretation. In order to understand and apply the canon correctly, some idea of the notion and nature of strict interpretation is necessary. An explanation of strict interpretation, with notations regarding its historical development, has already been given in Article II of Chapter I.[7] For the purposes of the present chapter it will be enough to recall some of its essential features.

Strict interpretation restricts the number of persons, cases or

---

[6] Cf. can. 17, § 1.

[7] Cf. *supra*, pp. 24-31.

things that are to be included within the proper meaning of words. It reduces that meaning to the narrowest confines that will still permit the words to have some effect under their proper meaning. Terms frequently have, within the scope of their proper connotation, a strict and a broad meaning, i.e., they may be understood in a narrow or wide sense. For example, the term "cleric" actually includes all who have received tonsure.[8] This is its widest meaning or extension. Taken in a narrow or strict sense it would exclude those who have episcopal consecration or who enjoy some special status, dignity or office. These would be Bishops, religious, canons, prelates, etc. Another example is the term "people." Understood according to its broad or widest meaning, it includes both laymen and clerics. In the strict sense, however, the extension of the term is limited so as to include only laymen. The strict and broad meaning of the word "people" as a legal term was carefully determined in a decretal of Pope Boniface VIII.[9] In this decretal, the Pontiff ordained that if clerics are interdicted, no penalty is thereby imposed on the people unless they are specifically mentioned. Thus, the decretal actually defines the strict or narrow meaning of the term "people."[10]

According to the majority of authors both before and after the Code, the proper meaning of words constitutes the limits within which strict and broad interpretation are possible. There are some authors, however, who maintain that the meaning intended by the legislator determines the limits. Although the latter agree that strict and broad interpretation will usually be within the proper meaning of terms, they maintain that there are times when the broad meaning of a term may actually go beyond the limits of its proper signification, or when its strict meaning will be so narrow as to depart altogether from the proper signification. As noted in Chapter I, Michiels is one of the chief advocates of this opinion, at least as far as the interpretation of law is concerned.[11] In his commentary on canon 50, however, he makes mention only

---

[8] Cf. can. 111, § 2.

[9] C. 16, *de sententia excommunicationis, suspensionis et interdicti,* V, 11, in VI.

[10] Cf. Roelker, "An Important Rule of Law," *The Jurist,* XVII (1957), 13.

[11] Cf. *supra,* pp. 30, 31.

of the proper meaning of the words as the meaning within which the strict or broad interpretation of rescripts may occur.

From what has been said in the foregoing chapters in regard to the general norms of interpretation, it would seem that the majority opinion is the only one tenable, at least where there is question of the strict and broad interpretation of rescripts. The conclusion reached in Part II was that rescripts are always to be interpreted in such a way as to be understood according to some proper meaning of the terms.[12] It follows necessarily, then, that strict and broad interpretation will always be within the proper meaning of the terms of a rescript.

ARTICLE III. CANON 50 AND THE LAW BEFORE THE CODE

Before considering in detail the various types of rescripts that are subject to strict interpretation, notice should be taken of the relation between Canon 50 and its counterpart in pre-Code law. As will be seen in the course of this and the subsequent chapter, the legislation contained in canon 50 is substantially the same as the law that existed before the Code.[13] Therefore, it must be understood according to the old law and in keeping with the interpretations already given by approved pre-Code canonists.[14]

No attempt will be made at this time to explain the pre-Code legislation on the strict and broad interpretation of rescripts. It will be referred to and commented on during the discussion of the various rescripts that are subject to one or the other of these two types of interpretation. What should be noted at present is the fact that, while there is substantial agreement between the law of canon 50 and the law as it existed before the Code, the formula used by the legislator in expressing the present law is quite different in some respects and a considerable improvement over the old formula common among pre-Code authors.

The basis for the strict and broad interpretation of doubtful rescripts are the concepts expressed in the Rule of Law: *"Odia*

---

[12] Cf. *supra*, pp. 53, 54.

[13] Cf. Van Hove, *De Rescriptis,* n. 225; Michiels, *Normae Generales,* II, 429.

[14] Can. 6, n. 2.

restringi et favores convenit ampliari."[15] The rule is founded on the natural and reasonable idea that no one is expected to assume more obligations than necessary and, secondly, on the presumption that the benevolence of the legislator is to extend to the full amplitude of his concession.[16] Therefore, anything that is harmful, odious or disadvantageous should be minimized in favor of liberty and that which is favorable should be extended.

In using Rule 15 as a norm of interpretation, pre-Code authors went to great lengths to distinguish between odious and favorable rescripts. For the majority of them, a rescript was to be considered as odious or favorable depending upon its subject matter. They admitted, however, that when the favor in a rescript could not be distinguished from the *odium,* then the author's primary intention would have to be considered.[17] In general, they mentioned four categories of rescripts which they considered to be odious or harmful. They were: 1) rescripts *ad lites;* 2) rescripts injurious to the rights of others; 3) rescripts contrary to the law, and; 4) rescripts obtained for the purpose of acquiring possession of a benefice.[18] Except for number 3, the categories listed above are substantially the same as those contained in canon 50. It is especially in regard to rescripts contrary to the law that the wording of canon 50 differs from that used by authors before the Code. During the course of time, pre-Code canonists detected a number of failures on the part of Rule 15 as applied to rescripts contrary to the law. Although they continued to consider them as something odious and therefore subject to strict interpretation, they were forced to conclude that there were times when the rule did not hold. As a result, they began to note more and more exceptions when a broad, rather than a strict, interpretation would be warranted even though a rescript were contrary to the law.[19]

---

[15] Reg. 15, R. J. in VI.

[16] Cf. Roelker, *art. cit.,* p. 9.

[17] Cf. e.g., Reiffenstuel, *Tractatus de Regulis Juris,* Reg. 15, nn. 1-3.

[18] Cf. Suarez, *De Legibus,* lib. VIII, c. 27, nn. 2-9; Reiffenstuel, *Jus Canonicum Universum,* lib. I, tit. III, nn. 120-139; Grandclaude, *Jus Canonicum,* lib. V, sec. III, n. 1.

[19] Cf. especially Reiffenstuel, *Jus Canonicum Universum,* lib. I, tit. III, nn. 135-139.

In addition to these exceptions when certain types of rescripts should be broadly interpreted, the same authors make repeated mention of one type of rescript in particular which they considered to be favorable. They referred to this species of rescript as one which grants a *purum beneficium,* or *beneficium* in the strict sense. Such a rescript, according to them, is one that grants a favor that is not contrary to the law nor injurious to the rights of others, and therefore should be given a broad interpretation.[20]

In canon 50, the legislator of the Code avoids altogether the use of the terms "odious" and "favorable" with respect to rescripts that are to receive a strict or broad interpretation. Instead, he gives a taxative enumeration of those rescripts that are to be strictly interpreted and concludes by stating that all other rescripts are to be interpreted broadly. The formula which the legislator uses to express the law constitutes a marked change when compared with that used by authors prior to the Code. As will be seen more clearly in the course of this chapter, the introduction of the phrase *"in commodum privatorum"* is the major innovation which distinguishes the present law from the old one. It enables the legislator to avoid mention of the many *fallentiae* and exceptions with which the pre-Code authors were so occupied. By adding the phrase to the notion of rescript contrary to the law he eliminates the necessity for noting them.

In addition to rescripts *"quae adversantur legi in commodum privatorum,"* canon 50 lists three other categories of rescripts that are to be strictly interpreted. As the wording of the canon clearly indicates, these and only these four types of rescripts are subject to such interpretation. No mention is made in the canon of any particular type of rescript that is to be broadly interpreted. In this respect, also, the terminology of the canon differs from the pre-Code formula. The legislator simply directs that all other rescripts are to receive a broad interpretation.

The formula adopted by the legislator in canon 50 was chosen as the best available for expressing the pre-Code legislation on the strict and broad interpretation of rescripts. It offers nothing new

---

[20] Cf. Suarez, *op. cit.,* lib. VIII, c. 27, n. 2; Reiffenstuel, *op. cit.,* lib. I, tit. III, n. 127.

in the way of law. In the final analysis, it is only a restatement in somewhat different terminology of the law as it existed before the Code. As a legal enactment, the canon as stated may be looked upon as an improvement over its pre-Code counterpart. However, since no simple formula can be devised for adequately expressing the various rescripts that are subject to strict interpretation, canon 50 still requires some interpretation in order to understand it fully. It can be understood correctly only in the light of the law as it existed before the Code and with the aid of the interpretations given by approved pre-Code authors.

ARTICLE IV. RESCRIPTS SUBJECT TO STRICT INTERPRETATION

Section 1. Rescripts That Refer to Litigation

Of the various types of rescripts subject to strict interpretation, canon 50 mentions, first of all, rescripts that refer to litigation. In order to understand this provision of the canon, it is necessary to have some idea of the nature of rescripts *ad lites*. In general, they are rescripts that pertain to legal suits and to the administration of justice. For the latter reason, they are also referred to as rescripts of justice (*rescripta iustitiae*). Their chief purpose is to safeguard and protect the rights of the parties involved in a legal dispute.

Rescripts *ad lites* may be rescripts appointing judges, delegating jurisdiction, consigning a cause, permitting or ordering criminal prosecution, granting the *restitutio in integrum* and the like.[21] They are distinguished from other types of rescripts, especially rescripts of favor (*rescripta gratiae*), by reason of the fact that they are concerned solely and primarily with contentious matters, litigation and the vindication of rights. In short, they are rescripts that contain instructions, regulations, provisions or even decisions for the settlement of disputes, whether judicial or extrajudicial.

In nearly all cases, rescripts *ad lites* will be *secundum ius*. The reason for this is the fact that they are issued to safeguard the rights of individuals and moral persons, rights that are determined, for the most part, by law. Hence, the intention of the superior

---

[21] Cf. Cicognani, *Canon Law*, p. 738; Michiels, *op. cit.*, II, 429.

who issues such a reply will be to settle the matter under dispute according to the prescriptions of law.[22]

The regulation of canon 50 concerning the strict interpretation of rescripts that refer to litigation has been incorporated into the Code directly and almost verbatim from pre-Code jurisprudence and doctrine. One of the earliest and clearest statements of the principle upon which the law is based is found in a canon of the IV Lateran Council (1215) in which Pope Innocent III (1198-1216) ordained: *"lites restringendae sint potius quam laxandae."*[23] The canon was later inserted in the decretal collection of Pope Gregory IX (1227-1241).[24]

In his treatise on the interpretation of rescripts, Hostiensis simply quotes the principle to prove that, in doubt, a rescript involving some controversial matter should be strictly interpreted.[25] Other pre-Code authors not only cite the principle, but give a number of reasons why such rescripts should receive a strict interpretation. They point out the fact that rescripts *ad lites* curtail the exercise of ordinary power, i.e., the power which belongs by law to certain judges. For this reason, they argue, rescripts that involve litigation should be looked upon as something odious. The same authors also mention the fact that such rescripts contain matter which may occasion further disputes and, as a result, new litigation. In addition, while rescripts *ad lites* may prove beneficial to the party in whose favor a dispute is settled, they are to be looked upon as being unfavorable to the party that loses. For these reasons also, the authors conclude, the rescripts under discussion are to be classified as odious, or harmful, even though they are issued to further the observance of the law. Hence, they are to be strictly interpreted according to the rule: *"Odia restringi et favores convenit ampliari."*[26]

---

[22] For a more detailed description of rescripts *ad lites,* cf. *supra,* pp. 41-44.

[23] C. 37—Hardouin, vol. 7, 47.

[24] C. 28, X, *de rescriptis,* I, 3.

[25] *Summa Aurea,* lib. I, *De Rescriptis et eorum interpretatione,* n. 17.

[26] Cf. Panormitanus, *Commentaria,* lib. I, tit. III, c. 10, n. 3; lib. V, tit. XL, c. 16, n. 7; Fagnanus, *Commentaria Super Quinque Libros Decretalium* (5 vols. in 4, Venetiis, 1709), lib. V, tit. XL, c. 16, nn. 28-30 (hereafter cited *Commentaria*); Reiffenstuel, *op. cit.,* lib. I, tit. III, n. 121; Ferraris, *Prompta Bibliotheca,* VI, "Recriptum," n. 19.

In addition to the fact that rescripts *ad lites* are to be considered as something odious, pre-Code authors mention another reason why they should be strictly interpreted. Since they are usually *secundum ius,* they should be understood according to the prescriptions of the law. Therefore, whenever there is doubt as to the meaning of such a rescript, it should be strictly interpreted, if necessary, in order to prevent any deviation from the law.[27]

In commenting on canon 50 and the regulation concerning the strict interpretation of rescripts that refer to litigation, modern authors merely repeat the reasons given by pre-Code canonists as noted in the previous two paragraphs.[28] Since the canon itself offers nothing new in the way of law as far as rescripts *ad lites* are concerned, the proper understanding of the law should be sought in the writings of the pre-Code canonists. The reasons proposed by them for the strict interpretation of rescript *ad lites* are still valid.

The ultimate reason for narrowing the proper meaning of the term of such a rescript, and thus limiting the number of persons, cases or things that are to be included within its scope, is the fact that an *odium* of some sort is usually involved. The rescript itself is pointed toward the settlement of a controversy. One or the

---

[27] Cf. Barbosa, *Collectanea Doctorum tam Veterum quam Recentiorum in Ius Pontificium Universum* (4 vols., Lugduni, 1656), lib. I, tit. III, c. 18, n. 2 (hereafter cited *Collectanea*) ; Pirhing, *Jus Canonicum,* lib. I, tit. III, n. 15, Assertio 1; Reiffenstuel, *op. cit.,* lib. I, tit. III, n. 120. Pirhing and Reiffenstuel go so far as to say that, in doubt, a rescript of justice is to be understood according to the law, even if this has to be done "per impropriationem verborum, ac transpositionem clausularum." In view of what has been said in Chapter V on restrictive interpretation, such a position does not appear to be tenable under the Code law in canon 49. Although a rescript of justice, or rescript *ad lites,* will usually be *secundum ius,* nevertheless, if the proper meaning of the terms, taken in their narrow, or strict sense, involves some departure from the common law, then this meaning of the words must be understood as the one intended by the author of the rescript.—cf. *supra,* pp. 98-102; cf. also Michiels, *op. cit.,* II, 429, footnote, n. 4.

[28] Cf. Cicognani, *op. cit.,* p. 738; Michiels, *op. cit.,* II, pp. 429-430; Van Hove, *De Rescriptis,* n. 226. Ojetti still retains the opinion that a doubtful rescript of justice must be understood in an improper sense whenever the proper meaning of terms would involve a departure from the *ius commune.* —*Commentarium,* I, 247.

other party in a dispute stands to suffer a loss. Individual rights are frequently in question. In the absence of the principle of restriction, higher authorities are forced to intervene in matters which should be settled by lesser authorities in virtue of this principle. These, as well as other unfavorable effects, either accompany or follow upon the issuance of a rescript which pertains to litigation or to the administration of justice.

Section 2. Rescripts Adverse to the Acquired Rights of Others

The second category of rescripts mentioned in canon 50 are those *"quae iura aliis quaesita laedant."* The canon ordains that, in doubt, rescripts adverse to the acquired rights of others are to be strictly interpreted. As stated, this provision of the canon seems to be clear enough, so that no misunderstanding is possible. Not all authors, however, agree as to the manner in which it should be interpreted. The main difficulty centers around the extent of the phrase *"iura aliis quaesita."* For the majority, the phrase is to be understood in the strict sense, so that only rescripts which are adverse to the acquired rights of others are to be included within the scope of canon 50.[29] For others, the phrase is to be given a broad meaning, so as to include not only the rescripts mentioned above, but all those as well that are adverse to any right of a third party, or prove to be in any way harmful, onerous or injurious to another.[30]

Before discussing in detail the two different interpretations of the phrase *"iura aliis quaesita,"* it would be well to have some idea of the pre-Code jurisprudence and doctrine relative to the question of the interpretation of rescripts adverse to the rights of others.

---

[29] Cf. especially Michiels, *op. cit.*, II, pp. 430-431; also Abbo-Hannan, *The Sacred Canons*, I, 81; Beste, *Introductio in Codicem*, p. 115; O'Neill, *Papal Rescripts of Favor*, pp. 103-104.

[30] Cf. in particular Van Hove, *De Rescriptis*, n. 227; also Badii, *Institutiones*, p. 69; Cicognani, *Commentarium ad Librum I Codics Juris Canonici*, recognatum et auctum a Staffa (2 vols., Romae: Buona Stampa, 1939-1942), II, 402.

A. The Law Before the Code

An examination of the law prior to the Code reveals that the Holy See, in issuing rescripts, was ever anxious to avoid injuring the rights of third parties. It is not always clear, however, whether this intendment applied to any and every right of a third party and to every kind of injury. Pope Alexander III (1159-1181), for example, in settling a dispute over the right to install a pastor in a particular church wrote, that it was not his intention to prejudice the rights of the bishop of the diocese.[31] Innocent III (1198-1216), in settling a dispute which had arisen over the interpretation of a clause in a rescript *ad lites,* declared that if the clause had been understood in such a way as to prejudice the other party in the case, then the decision in the case was invalid.[32] Pope Gregory IX (1227-1241), writing to the archdeacon of Lincoln, decreed that favors petitioned from the Holy See without mentioning the privileges held by others were invalid, and stated as a reason, the fact that the Holy See does not want to prejudice the rights of others.[33] In one of his letters ordering the restoration of a benefice, Boniface VIII (1294-1303) demanded that it be conferred without prejudice to the former incumbent.[34]

From the decretals noted above, it can be seen that the Pontiffs cited decreed, as a principle of law, that rescripts, especially rescripts granting favors, should be understood in such a way as to be prejudicial to no one. The same principle is expressed in more general terms in Rule 48 of the *Regulae Juris* in the *Liber Sextus.* According to that rule, no one ought to obtain an advantage with injury or loss to another.[35]

The decretalists and early commentators used this principle a great deal in discussing the interpretation of rescripts and privileges. In applying the principle, they often distinguished between rescripts prejudicial to the rights of a third person and those

---

[31] C. 15, X, *de officio et potestate iudicis delegati,* I, 29; Jaffé, n. 13842.

[32] C. 18, X, *de rescriptis,* I, 3; Potthast, n. 59.

[33] C. 31, X, *de privilegiis et excessibus privilegiatorum,* V, 33; Potthast, n. 9681.

[34] C. 8, *de rescriptis,* I, 3 in VI.

[35] "Locupletari non debet aliquis cum alterius iniuria vel iactura."

prejudicial to the author of the rescript. They considered rescripts prejudicial to the rights of a third party as something odious and therefore subject to strict interpretation, whenever there was real doubt as to the meaning intended in a rescript. Against the rights of the author of a rescript, they allowed a broad interpretation, inasmuch as the author was considered to have yielded his rights according to the stipulations of the rescript. An exception requiring strict interpretation was made, however, in regard to privileges granted by the Holy See. The writers classified a rescript as prejudicial to the rights of others, whenever it proved harmful, injurious or burdensome to another, or deprived some third person of a right that belonged to him by law. In general, the early authors held that a slight injury was to be overlooked, since a rescript granting a favor to one person often entails some loss on the part of another. Hence, only rescripts prejudicial to others in such a way as to cause some great harm or loss or injury were to be given a strict interpretation.[36]

In their treatises on the interpretation of rescripts and privileges, the later commentators continued to make use of the principle stated above, namely, a rescript or privilege should not be prejudicial to another. Whereas the majority of early authors held that a rescript would have to cause some notable or grave harm before a strict interpretation was demanded, later authors tended to stress the idea that even a slight injury or prejudice would be reason enough to warrant such an interpretation. There were some, however, who continued to follow the former opinion. Although most of the authors spoke of rights in general, and considered a rescript prejudicial or injurious to the right of another as something odious and therefore to be strictly interpreted, there are a number of canonists who mention only acquired rights when

---

[36] *Glossa ordinaria* ad c. 20, C. IX, q. 3, s.v. *privilegium;* c. 6, C. XXV, q. 2, s.v. *Servatis;* c. 15, C. XXV, q. 2, s.v. *Quod non laedat;* c. 7, X, de rescriptis, I, 3, s.v. *Intentionis;* Innocent IV, *Commentaria,* lib. V, tit. XL, c. 16; Hostiensis, *Summa Aurea,* lib. V, *De Privilegiis,* § 9; Panormitanus, *Commentaria,* lib. V, tit. XXXIII, c. 22, n. 3; lib. V, tit. XL, c. 28, n. 2; c. 32, n. 4; c. 16, n. 7. Cf. Van Hove, *Commentarium Lovaniense* I, Tom. V (*De Privilegiis, De Dispensationibus*) (Mechliniae, 1939), n. 184 (hereafter cited *De Privilegiis, De Dispensationibus*); Michiels, *op. cit.,* II, 573.

treating the question of the strict interpretation of rescripts or privileges.

Suarez, for example, has a discussion on the interpretation of privileges. He mentions therein that a privilege, prejudicial to a third person in such a way as to be contrary to a right which he has already acquired (*ius acquisitum*), is to be considered odious, and for that reason it should be restricted in so far as this can be done. He gives as a reason, the fact that it is not the intention of the one who grants the privilege to take away the right of another, unless he expressly declares this effect to be so. Even though a privilege be granted *motu proprio,* he contends, it is not to be extended so as to deprive another of a right which he has acquired. Suarez goes on to state, that it is a tenet of the common law, as well as of the natural law, that the right of each and every person be safeguarded and, although a superior can at times take this right away, he may not do so without a sufficient cause.[37] It is to be noted that Suarez makes mention of an acquired right only in connection with a privilege prejudicial to a third person. Although he states that such a privilege should be restricted rather than extended, he is actually speaking of strict and broad interpretation, as is evident from what he has to say earlier in his treatise.[38]

Cardinal Fagnanus (+ 1678) considers at some length the question of the interpretation of rescripts granting privileges that touch upon the rights of a third person. Such rescripts, he maintains, are to be interpreted in such a way as not to injure another or to prejudice his right. He states that, in general, the concessions of a superior are to be interpreted in a manner that will not prove injurious to a third party. This applies, he continues, even though a privilege be granted to a needy person, for the want of one person should not be relieved by injuring another. Fagnanus is of the opinion that, even though the injury done to another be slight, the rule still applies.[39]

---

[37] *De Legibus,* lib. VIII, c. 27, n. 9.

[38] *Ibid.*, n. 1. Cf. *supra,* pp. 25, 26.

[39] *Commentaria Super Quinque Libros Decretalium* (5 vols. in 4, Venetiis, 1709), lib. I, tit. 3, c. 18, nn. 10-15 (hereafter cited *Commentaria*).

Fagnanus is here apparently considering a right in general, for he makes no mention of an acquired right. Further on in his commentary, however, he does have something to say about the latter. He notes that where there is a question of taking away an acquired right from another, it does not suffice that the words of an Apostolic rescript be clear, or that the Pope have knowledge of this fact. Instead, there must be express mention and derogation of the rule which states that an acquired right is not to be taken away. Fagnanus adds, however, that the rule does not hold and, hence, no derogation is required in the case of a favor *"ex sua natura praejudiciali,"* or a favor that is granted for the public welfare. He gives no reasons for the exceptions which he makes.

In his classic commentary on the Rules of the Apostolic Chancery, Riganti (1661-1735) has some pertinent observations on rule 18 *"de non tollendo ius quaesitum."*[40] The rule states that all the various declarations, letters, mandates and concessions granted by the Apostolic See are to be interpreted so as not to harm the acquired rights of another. According to Riganti, the rule is derived from the various prescriptions of the law which ordain, that the concessions of a superior are to be so understood as not to be adverse to the rights of another, nor injure a third party. In his opinion, the rule holds good even though the injury done is slight, for the rule uses the word *"quomodolibet,"* which includes every acquired right however limited it may be. This is true, he adds, even though various glosses state the opposite. Like-

---

[40] According to Riganti, the rule was first issued by Benedict XIII (+ 1428) but was restricted at that time to favors pertaining to vacant benefices. Additions to the rule were made by successive Pontiffs until it took on the form of the rule which Riganti himself quotes: "Item ne per varias, quae pro commissionibus, seu mandatis, et declarationibus habendis in causis plerumque, fiunt, suggestiones, Iustitia postponatur: Idem Dominus Noster decrevit, et declaravit Suae intentionis fore quod deinceps per quamcumque Signaturam seu concessionem, aut gratiam, vel Litteras Apostolicas pro commissionibus, seu mandatis, aut declarationibus huiusmodi etiamsi Motu proprio, et ex certa scientia, ac etiam ante motam litem a Sanctitate Sua emanaverint, vel de eius mandato faciendas, nulli Ius sibi quaesitum quomodolibet tollatur."—*Commentaria in Regulas, Constitutiones et Ordinationes Cancellariae Apostolicae* (4 vols. in 2, Coloniae Allobrogum, 1751), Reg. XVIII, n . 1.

wise, he notes, the rule applies where a favor is granted *motu proprio,* and even though the clause *"ex certa scientia"* is included. So, too, in a favor granted to some needy person. The rule applies to any and every acquired right, whether the right is acquired by a particular indult, a statute, a privilege or by common law. Riganti states further that the rule is to be observed even though the Pope in issuing a declaration, or granting a favor, should know that what he is granting will be prejudicial to a third party. In such a case, he concludes, a grant of a favor will always be invalid unless the right already acquired by the first person in the matter is taken away.[41]

Pirhing holds the opinion that, in doubt, one is never to presume that the author of a rescript intends that his reply be understood so as to be harmful to another *"saltem graviter seu enormiter."* He mentions that a slight injury or prejudice to the rights of another may be overlooked. He makes no mention of an acquired right, but merely speaks in general terms of injury or prejudice to another.[42]

In his discussion of the interpretation of rescripts and privileges, Reiffenstuel notes that, in doubt, a privilege that is prejudicial to the right of another is to be understood *"civiliter et temperate,"* so as to cause the least possible harm. Therefore, he concludes, a strict interpretation must be given. He makes no attempt, at least here, to explain what he means by a privilege prejudicial to the right of another.[43] However, in his commentary on the Rule of Law: *"Odia restringi et favores convenit ampliari,"* he states that the section of the rule calling for extension in favorable matters fails in the interpretation of any and every enactment, even though it may be considered especially favorable, whenever there is prejudice to the acquired right of a third person.[44] Of particular interest are the sources which Reiffenstuel cites as the basis for this exception. He cites, first of all, the letter of Alexander III referred to earlier and from which the commentators deduce the rule that

---

[41] *Ibid.,* nn. 3-17.
[42] *Jus Canonicum,* lib. I, tit. III, n. 39.
[43] *Jus Canonicum Universum,* lib. I, tit. III, n. 132.
[44] *Tractatus de Regulis Juris,* Reg. 15, n. 26.

a rescript should not be prejudicial to another.[45] Secondly, he cites the rule of the Apostolic Chancery *"de non tollendo ius quaesitum."* While he gives no further explanation, the implication is that the two rules taken together prove that, although a rescript or other legal enactment that grants a favor should ordinarily be broadly interpreted, by way of exception it will have to be given a strict interpretation whenever it is prejudicial to the acquired right of a third party.

What is implied in Reiffenstuel's commentary on Rule 15 is clearly stated by Leurenius in his commentary on the decretals of Gregory IX. In that section of his commentary that has a direct bearing on the question under discussion, Leurenius mentions by way of introduction that, in doubt, that interpretation is to be preferred which does not lessen in any way the acquired right of another. He follows by stating that the rule applies not only in contracts and testaments, but also in privileges and rescripts, even though such clauses as *"ex certa scientia"* and *"motu proprio"* are inserted. The rule applies, according to him, because the phrase *"salvo iure tertii"* or *"sine praeiudicio tertii"* is always understood in all such documents. It would seem, then, that Leurenius restricts the meaning of the term *"ius"* in these two phrases to include only an acquired right.[46]

From the foregoing survey of pre-Code jurisprudence and doctrine, the following conclusions may be drawn. Where there is a question of an acquired right, that right must be expressly abrogated before a rescript granted to another person and touching upon that right will be effective. If the rescript does contain such an abrogating clause, but the meaning of the words of the rescript are not clear, then a strict interpretation must be given. This conclusion seems certain in view of the Rule of the Apostolic Chancery *"de non tollendo ius quaesitum."*

Where there is a question of a rescript adverse to rights other than acquired rights, neither the pre-Code law nor the teaching of

---

[45] C. 15, X, *de officio et potestate iudicis delegati,* I, 29. Cf. *supra,* p. 118.

[46] *Forum Ecclesiasticum in quo Jus Canonicum Universum Librorum ac Titulorum ordine explanatur* (5 vols. in 3, Venetiis, 1729), lib. V, tit. XL, n. 5.

canonists is altogether clear. The most that can be said is that the law states that a rescript is not to be understood in such a way as to be prejudicial to another. Some authors understand this rule to mean that, in doubt, a rescript that proves to be in any way, even slightly, prejudicial, harmful or injurious to the rights of another is to be strictly interpreted. Others maintain that the injury, prejudice or harm must be notable before a strict interpretation is required. For the most part, the authors speak only of a right in general, and make no mention of acquired right as such. There are several, however, notably Suarez and Leurenius, and even Reiffenstuel, who seem to understand the law as applying only to rescripts, privileges, etc., that are adverse to the acquired rights of others.

B. The Law of the Code

In Canon 50, the legislator of the Code mentions specifically rescripts *"quae iura aliis quaesita laedunt* as one of the species of rescripts that are subject to strict interpretation in case of doubt. Van Hove is of the opinion that the *ius quaesitum* of canon 50 is not to be understood in the strict sense in which it is used in canon 46, but is to be understood in the broad sense as referring to rescripts and privileges which prove to be in any way harmful, burdensome or injurious to others.[47] According to him, it does not matter whether the primary intention of the author of a rescript is to grant a favor to one person or impose a burden on another. If a rescript or privilege is favorable to one person and injurious, harmful or burdensome to another, it is to be strictly interpreted. Van Hove, then, not only adopts the rule that a doubtful rescript should be understood in such a way as not to be prejudicial to another, but believes that the rule is included in the present legislation of canon 50.

Michiels takes exception to the view held by Van Hove on the grounds that such an interpretation is alien to the mind of the

---

[47] "Ius quaesitum autem non est intelligendum sensu stricto quo sumitur in c. 46. Agitur de rescriptis et privilegiis quae sint aliis odiosa, quia onera eis imponunt aut incommodum generant aut illos gravant . . ."—*De Rescriptis,* n. 227.

legislator, inasmuch as it is obviously contrary to the juridical meaning of the expression that is used in canon 50. He agrees that there is some foundation for the strict interpretation of all rescripts that are harmful to others, but it is his contention that, if such a rule is to be admitted, it has its source in the natural law and does not derive from the positive legislation of canon 50.[48]

One cannot ignore the fact that, in canon 50, the legislator speaks only of rescripts that are adverse to the acquired rights of others. This writer is of the opinion that, if the legislator intended to include in the canon not only rescripts adverse to acquired rights but those injurious to any and all rights, he would have made known this intention, especially in view of pre-Code doctrine stated above, by using an expression such as "rescripts injurious to the right of another" or "rescripts prejudicial to a third person." One or the other of these two phrases would be broad enough to include all rights in general. The term *"ius quaesitum"* has its own proper juridical meaning, which is limited in its scope. While authors do not agree as to the exact definition of an acquired right, they do agree that there are certain conditions which must be fulfilled before a right can be designated as a vested or acquired right. First, there must be some norm of law by virtue of which the specific right in question can be acquired; secondly, a juridical fact must have taken place, by which the right has been actually acquired.[49] An acquired right, then, is more than a mere capacity or right to act which one may have in virtue of the law. It is the right which comes into the possession of a person in virtue of some juridical fact that has been performed and completed by that person while still retaining his general capacity to act under the law. Thus, the right to marry which one may have by law becomes an acquired right once marriage is validly contracted. The valid marriage contract is the juridic fact in virtue of which the previous general capacity or right to marry is transformed into a vested or acquired right.

---

[48] *Op. cit.*, II, 431.

[49] Bouscaren-Ellis, *Canon Law*, p. 19; Coronata, *Institutiones*, I, pp. 6, 7; Frison, *The Retroactivity of Law*, The Catholic University of America Canon Law Studies, n. 231 (Washington, D. C.: The Catholic University of America Press, 1946), p. 112.

According to the commonly accepted meaning of the term, an acquired right is had only when the two conditions mentioned above have been fulfilled. Canon 18 directs that ecclesiastical laws are to be understood according to the proper meaning of their terms. Therefore, the expression *"iura aliis quaesita"* in canon 50 should be understood according to its proper and commonly accepted meaning. Contrary to what Van Hove says, it does not include rights in general. The same expression is used in canon 46 as well as canon 4. Van Hove, himself, admits that its meaning in canon 46 is restricted to acquired rights. There is no juridically acceptable reason for understanding it otherwise in canon 50.

What then of the pre-Code rule concerning the interpretation of rescripts prejudicial to the rights of another? In so far as it applies to rescripts adverse to the acquired rights of others, it is included within the scope of canon 50. In so far as the rule pertains to rescripts that are prejudicial to rights other than acquired rights, the Code makes no mention of it in canon 50. The legislator has seen fit to retain the principle as a piece of positive legislation only in so far as it applies to rescripts adverse to acquired rights of others. As Michiels points out, justice may at times demand that a rescript be understood in such a way as not to be harmful or injurious to another. This, however, is a problem for the moralist rather than the canonist. The Code is concerned only with rescripts adverse to the acquired rights of others. According to canon 50, in doubt, such rescripts are to receive a strict interpretation. Before using this norm, however, the provisions of canon 46 should be taken into consideration.

Canon 46 also makes mention of rescripts that are adverse to the acquired rights of others. The canon ordains that, unless an express derogatory clause is appended to such a rescript, it will not be sustained even though it be granted *motu proprio.*[50] Hence, before a rescript contrary to the acquired right of a third person

[50] "Rescripta etiam Motu proprio concessa de iure communi inhabili ad consequendam gratiam de qua agitur, itemque edita contra alicuius loci legitimam consuetudinem vel statutum peculiare, vel contra ius alteri iam quaesitum, non sustinentur, nisi expressa derogatoria clausula rescripto apponatur."

can be effective, the rescript must contain a clause expressly abrogating the right in question or at least modifying it (*derogatoria clausula*). The grantor must state in explicit terms that he is removing such a right. The Canon does not state that rescripts contrary to the acquired rights of others are absolutely invalid, but rather that they will not be sustained. The party possessing the acquired right may consent to the granting or use of a rescript against his right. If such is the case, the rescript should be considered effective in practice.

According to Michiels, the special norm of canon 50 under consideration in this section is applicable only to rescripts adverse to the acquired rights of others to which the express derogatory clause of canon 46 is appended. As a reason, he simply states that without the clause rescripts opposed to the acquired rights of others will not be sustained.[51] It would seem, however, that the norm of canon 50 in relation to canon 46 is applicable whether or not rescripts adverse to the acquired rights of others contain a derogating clause. There is a manifest difference between interpretation (canon 50) and use (canon 46). For one thing, canon 50 clearly states that doubtful rescripts, *"quae iura aliis quaesita laedunt,"* are to be strictly interpreted. The wording of the canon seems to indicate that all such rescripts are subject to strict interpretation. The fact that a rescript adverse to another's acquired right does not contain a clause abrogating that right does not necessarily mean that a strict interpretation would be superfluous. It could happen that by interpreting such a rescript strictly no harm would be done to the other party's acquired right. As a result, canon 46 would no longer apply.

Moreover, if the party who stands to suffer a loss consents to the use of a rescript against his acquired right, the rescript is thereby made effective. Is one to suppose that such a rescript is not subject to strict interpretation merely because it contains no derogatory clause? On the contrary, the special norm of canon 50 would have to be used. In this writer's opinion, all doubtful rescript adverse to the acquired rights of others must be strictly

---

[51] *Normae Generales,* II, 430; cf. also Roelker, "An Important Rule of Law," *The Jurist,* XVII (1957), 21.

interpreted. If, after such an interpretation, a particular rescript remains opposed to another's acquired right, canon 46 becomes applicable. The rescript will not be sustained unless there is appended to it a clause expressly derogating the acquired right in question; or unless the third party can and does waive his vested right.

Section 3. Rescripts Which Grant to Private Persons Favors Against the Law

Among rescripts subject to strict interpretation in case of doubt, canon 50 mentions those *"quae adversantur legi in commodum privatorum."* The canon directs that, in doubt, rescripts that grant to private persons favors against the law are to receive a strict interpretation. As a special norm for the interpretation of rescripts, this particular provision of Canon 50 is concerned only with rescripts that grant favors contrary to or in opposition to the law. It is important to note that the canon does not state that all doubtful rescripts that are contrary to the law are to be strictly interpreted, but only those that are contrary to the law in such a way as to favor private persons. In order to understand this disposition of canon 50, then, it is necessary to have a clear notion of the meaning of the phrase *"in commodum privatorum."* The phrase can best be understood by examining the law as it existed before the Code.

As will be seen, the legislation of canon 50 regarding the strict interpretation of rescripts contrary to the law in favor of private persons is but a restatement of pre-Code jurisprudence and doctrine. It must be interpreted, then, upon the authority of the old law and in accord with the interpretations of that law as given by approved pre-Code authors.[52] The only difference between the law before the Code and the present legislation is the manner in which the law is expressed. The formula used by the legislator in canon 50 in expressing the law is much more simple and direct, as can be seen when compared with the law as stated before the Code.

---

[52] Can. 6, n. 2.

A. The Law Before the Code

The pre-Code discipline regarding the interpretation of rescripts that grant favors contrary to the law may be summarized as follows. In general, every departure or exception to law was looked upon as something unfavorable, as an *odium* in regard to the law and, as a result, as something to be restricted as far as interpretation was concerned. This is the fundamental principle which forms the basis for the strict interpretation of rescripts, privileges, dispensations and all other similar legal enactments that are contrary to the law. The principle is clearly enunciated by Boniface VIII in one of his letters. Speaking of a certain dispensation, he wrote that "superseding the law, it ought to be restricted as something odious."[53] The same principle is found in the axiom: *"Quae a jure communi exorbitant, nequaquam ad consequentiam sunt trahenda."*[54] According to this rule, exceptions to the provisions of the common law should never be drawn into precedents. In other words, they should not be considered as examples to be followed. They are not to be extended so as to include other persons, cases or things. Not only are they not to be extended, they are to be restricted.[55]

Pre-Code authors cite the above letter and rule, as well as Rule 15 of the *Regulae Iuris*,[56] as the main sources for the strict interpretation of rescripts granting favors contrary to the law. Many simply mention the fact that such rescripts are odious, unfavorable or harmful, since they depart from the law, and for that reason they should be strictly interpreted.[57] Others explain more fully why rescripts granting favors contrary to the law are odious or unfavorable. Thus, Reiffenstuel is careful to point out that, although rescripts granting privileges contrary to the law contain a favor, they are to be strictly interpreted because the favor that they contain is merely a private one *"cui praeponderat favor juris*

[53] C. 1, *de filiis presbyterorum,* I, 11 in VI.

[54] Reg. 28, R. J. in VI.

[55] *Glossa ordinaria* ad Reg. 28, R. J. in VI.

[56] "Odia restringi et favores convenit ampliari."

[57] Cf. Suarez, *De Legibus,* lib. VIII, c. 27, n. 5; Schmalzgrueber, *Jus Ecclesiasticum Universum,* lib. V, tit. XXXIII, n. 125; Ferraris, *Prompta Bibliotheca,* V, "Privilegium," n. 28.

communis."[58] Grandclaude notes that privileges contrary to the law are to be strictly interpreted because the common law is ordained for the common good and the public welfare, and, therefore, anything that detracts from the law is odious.[59] The idea which he has in mind is the fact that the common good and the public welfare are protected by the law. Anything that weakens this protection is unfavorable to the common good and the public welfare. Privileges opposed to the law tend to weaken the protection afforded by the law. For this reason, in particular, they are unfavorable and should receive a strict interpretation whenever there is any doubt as to their meaning.

Following the principle that every departure or exception to the provisions of the law was an *odium* in regard to the law, pre-Code authors were inclined to consider all rescripts contrary to the law as unfavorable and therefore subject to strict interpretation. They realized, however, that there were certain exceptions to the rule, certain instances when a broad rather than a strict interpretation was warranted, even though a doubtful rescript contained a favor that was opposed to the law. Actually, the principle applies only when rescripts, dispensations, privileges and the like are opposed to the law *in commodum privatorum*. That pre-Code canonists were aware of this concept of the principle, at least indirectly, is evident from the many exceptions and failures which they mention. Instead of stating that only rescripts opposed to the law in such a way as to favor private persons are subject to strict interpretation, they began by noting that all rescripts contrary to the law should be restricted as something odious. They then proceeded to give the various exceptions to the rule. From the exceptions that they mention, it can be seen that only rescripts that grant favors to private persons are subject to strict interpretation in case of doubt. This is the law as it is expressed in canon 50.

Some mention should be made of the principal exceptions which are noted and discussed by pre-Code canonists. A brief summary of these exceptions will help to explain the meaning of the phrase

---

[58] *Tractatus De Regulis Juris*, Reg. 15, n. 11; *Jus Canonicum Universum*, lib. I, tit. III, n. 133.

[59] *Jus Canonicum*, lib. V, sec. III, n. 1.

"in commodum privatorum" and will show how the special norm under consideration in this section is to be understood and applied. Among the exceptions to the general rule calling for the strict interpretation of rescripts that grant favors contrary to the law, pre-Code authors mention in particular rescripts that favor religion and those that favor the common good.

The principal source for the exception made in favor of religion is a letter of Pope Honorius III (1216-1227).[60] Honorius had granted to the Order of Preachers and the Friars Minor the privilege of celebrating Mass at any place on a portable altar, provided that the privilege was not used in a way that would infringe upon parish rights. Some had given too strict an interpretation to the grant and held that the recipients could not use the privilege without the consent of the local prelates. In a letter to the Bishop of Paris, the Pontiff began by stating that, in matters which are intended to promote divine worship, a "benign" rather that a "malign" interpretation should be given. He expressed surprise over the fact that some had interpreted his grant too strictly, and, having voiced his disapproval and reprobation of such an interpretation, he ordered the privilege to be interpreted in a manner that would enable the friars to obtain some benefit from his good will in the matter. Of interest at the moment is the principle which he laid down in the very beginning of his letter, that in matters which are intended to promote divine worship a "benign" interpretation should be given. In using the term "benign" he evidently means a broad interpretation, for he expresses his disapproval of the strict interpretation which the privilege had received.

In his treatise on the sacrament of matrimony, Sanchez (+ 1610) treats extensively the subject of dispensations and dwells at some length on the question of their interpretation.[61] What he has to say on the subject is applicable to the interpretation of rescripts which make concessions or grant favors contrary

---

[60] C. 30, X, *de privilegiis et excessibus privilegiatorum,* V, 33; Potthast, n. 7467.

[61] *De Sancto Matrimonii Sacramento Disputationum Libri Tres* (3 vols. in 1, Venetiis, 1726), lib. VIII, disp. 1 (hereafter cited *De Matrimonio*).

to the law. After defining a dispensation as a "relaxation of a law made by one having the power to relax the law," he concludes almost immediately, that a dispensation is thus to be strictly interpreted since it departs from the *ius commune*.[62] Further on, however, in discussing the various exceptions to the above rule, he states that the rule is to be understood as applying only to dispensations and privileges that are granted to private persons. According to him, privileges granted to a whole religious community are to be given a broad interpretation as being something favorable.[63]

According to Suarez, privileges granted in favor of religion or some pious cause, as well as those that are considered necessary for the common good of the State, are always to receive a broad interpretation. By way of example he mentions privileges granted to soldiers, the privilege of exempting clerics from temporal jurisdiction, or religious from the jurisdiction of the Ordinary. Even though such privileges be contrary to the law, he notes, they are to be broadly interpreted in favor of religion or the common good of the State. The reason why privileges of this nature are not to be restricted, according to him, is that the good done to religion in general, or to some pious cause or to the State, is thought to outweigh the evil which ordinarily results from deviation or departure from the common law. Moreover, he adds, one may prudently conjecture that this is the intention of the one granting the privileges.[64]

According to Reiffenstuel, rescripts and privileges contrary to the law are to be given a broad rather than a strict interpretation whenever they grant favors in behalf of the public welfare, divine worship, the faith, religion in general or the salvation of souls. He adds further that, according to some authors,[65] a broad interpretation is permitted in regard to concessions made in favor of a church, monastery, hospital or other pious cause.[66]

---

[62] *Ibid.*, nn. 2, 3.

[63] *Ibid.*, n. 13.

[64] *Op. cit.*, lib. VIII, c. 27, n. 7.

[65] He cites by name Sylvester, Suarez and Laymann.

[66] *Tractatus De Regulis Juris*, Reg. 15, nn. 20, 21; cf. also *Jus Canonicum Universum*, lib. I, tit. III, n. 138.

Pre-Code authors also excepted *motu proprio* rescripts from the general rule requiring the strict interpretation of rescripts contrary to the law. There is no law in the *Corpus Iuris Canonici* which expressly states that *motu proprio* rescripts contrary to the law are to receive a broad interpretation. Boniface VIII, however, declared as a principle of law that a *motu proprio* rescript obtained for the purpose of acquiring an ecclesiastical benefice should be broadly interpreted. This ruling was an exception to the general rule calling for the strict interpretation of such rescripts.[67] Pre-Code canonists applied the ruling to rescripts granting privileges and favors contrary to the law. Suarez, for example, cites it to prove that privileges granted *motu proprio* are to be given a broad rather than a strict interpretation, even though they are contrary to the law. According to him, such a privilege is to be thought of as a *beneficium*, or favor, in the strict sense. It is granted *ex certa scientia*. Therefore, in doubt, it should be extended rather than restricted.[68] Commentators after Suarez merely repeat what he has to say in the matter.[69] Suarez speaks of *motu proprio* privileges in general and makes no distinction between those granted for the benefit of private persons and those which favor the common good. It would seem that he, as well the later commentators in general, considered all *motu proprio* rescripts, privileges and dispensations as meriting a broad interpretation. According to the earlier commentators, it would seem that only those granted for the common good could be given such an interpretation.[70]

Another exception mentioned by pre-Code authors has to do with the interpretation of rescripts that are contrary to a particular status or custom. It was the common opinion among canonists before the Code that the rule calling for the strict interpretation of rescripts contrary to the law applied also to rescripts that granted

[67] C. 23, 24, *de praebendis et dignitatibus,* III, 4 in VI.

[68] *Op. cit.,* lib. VIII, c. 27, n. 8.

[69] Cf. Reiffenstuel, *Jus Canonicum Universum,* lib. I, tit. III, n. 139; Schmalzgrueber, *Jus Ecclesiasticum Universum,* lib. V, tit. XXXIII, n. 126. Cf. also Van Hove, *De Privilegiis, De Dispensationibus,* n. 189.

[70] Felinus, *Commentaria,* lib. I, tit. III, c. 27, n. 13; Sanchez, *De Matrimonio,* lib. VIII, disp. 1, n. 5. Cf. Van Hove, *loc. cit.*

favors that were opposed to a particular statute or custom.[71] However, rescripts opposed to a particular statute or custom in such a way as to effect a return to the provisions of the common law were looked upon as something favorable. Therefore, they were interpreted broadly inasmuch as they furthered the observance of the *ius commune*.[72]

Before considering the law of the Code, one further pre-Code principle affecting the interpretation of rescripts granting privileges contrary to the law must be noted. Although privileges contrary to the law were deemed unfavorable, according to pre-Code discipline, they were never to be so strictly interpreted as to be useless or without effect. This principle as a norm for the interpretation of privileges derives mainly from the letter of Pope Honorius III already referred to previously. In this particular letter, Honorius expressed his disapproval over the fact that the privilege of celebrating Mass on a portable altar which he had granted to the Order of Preachers and the Friars Minor had been too strictly interpreted. He wrote that, as a result of the strict interpretation, those who had received the privilege were not permitted to celebrate Mass in accordance with the Apostolic grant. He ordered the privilege to be interpreted in a manner that would enable the recipients to obtain some benefit from his good will in the matter. At the same time he cautioned the Friars to abstain from whatever might be injurious to parish rights.[73]

In commenting on this letter, the glossator observes that a favor ought always to grant something, for otherwise it would be a mere delusion.[74] His words are similar to those used by Boniface VIII in one of his letters in which he wrote that words ought to have some effect in documents which grant privileges and special favors.[75]

---

[71] Suarez, *op. cit.*, lib. VIII, c. 28, n. 8; Schmalzgrueber, *op. cit.*, lib. V, tit. XXXIII, n. 127.

[72] Panormitanus, *Commentaria*, lib. V, tit. XL, c. 16, n. 6; Felinus, *Commentaria*, lib. I, tit. III, c. 18, n. 11; Sanchez, *op. cit.*, lib. VIII, disp. 1, n. 12; Schmalzgrueber, *op. cit.*, lib. V, tit. XXXIII, n. 127.

[73] C. 30, X, *de privilegiis et excessibus privilegiatorum*, V, 33.

[74] *Glossa ordinaria*, s.v *Ex indulgentia*.

[75] C. 10, *de privilegiis*, V, 7 in VI.

According to Suarez, a privilege is never to be so strictly interpreted as to be useless or without effect, no matter how harmful or odious it should appear, provided, however, that it is not unjust. He gives as a reason the fact that the will of the one granting the privilege should not be thwarted, nor rendered ineffectual. Just as a law should not be interpreted in such a way as to render it useless, since this would be contrary to the intention of the lawgiver who does not legislate without reason, so, according to Suarez, a privilege should not be so restricted as to render it useless. This is true, he adds, even though a privilege be extended to that which appeared to be against the law. He concludes by stating that, if necessary, a privilege may be extended beyond the proper meaning of its words in order to prevent a person from being deprived of the favor that is granted him.[76]

Suarez' interpretation of the special norm which directs that a privilege should have some effect reflects the doctrine common among pre-Code canonists.[77] It should be noted, however, that some authors apply the principle to dispensations as well as privileges. Sanchez, for example, mentions that a dispensation is to be strictly interpreted, but in a way that will allow it to have some effect. It is never to be so strictly interpreted as to be a mere illusion.[78]

B. *The Law of the Code*

The present law of the Code regarding the interpretation of doubtful rescripts contrary to the law is found chiefly in canon 50. The canon states that, in doubt, rescripts opposed to the law *in commodum privatorum* are to be strictly interpreted. No express

[76] Suarez is here considering privileges in general, whether they are merely beyond the law or contrary to the law. In either case, according to him, they are to be interpreted so as to give some effect to the grant.—*op. cit.,* lib. VIII, c. 28, n. 2. Cf. Panormitanus, *Commentaria,* lib. V, tit. XL, c. 25, n. 6.

[77] Fagnanus, *Commentaria,* lib. V, tit. XL, c. 16, n. 24; Reiffenstuel, *Jus Canonicum Universum,* lib. I, tit. III, n. 137; Schmalzgrueber, *op. cit.,* lib. V, tit. XXXIII, n. 122.

[78] *Op. cit.,* lib. VIII, disp. 1, nn. 3, 16. Cf. also Schmalzgrueber, *op. cit.,* lib. I, tit. III, n. 30.

mention is made of any other type of rescript that may be contrary to the law. As far as canon 50 is concerned, in doubt, only rescripts opposed to the law *in commodum privatorum* are to receive a strict interpretation. All other doubtful rescripts opposed to the law, but not *in commodum privatorum,* are to be broadly interpreted, unless they refer to litigation, are adverse to the acquired rights of others or are obtained for the purpose of acquiring an ecclesiastical benefice.

Rescripts opposed to the law *in commodum privatorum* are those that favor private persons. They contain privileges, dispensations and the like. They are to be strictly interpreted because they contain an exception to the law which favors private persons at the expense of the common good. As seen in the previous subdivision, the common good is protected by the law. Whatever may weaken this protection is unfavorable to the common good.[79] Rescripts opposed to the law in favor of private persons are injurious to the law. They remove persons from the general obligation of the law involved and, as a result, weaken the protection afforded the common good by the law.

Rescripts opposed to the law, but not *in commodum privatorum,* are not so characterized. They are rescripts that favor the public good rather than private persons. Canon 50 does not specifically mention this type of rescript. Commentators before the Code devoted considerable time and space to a consideration of them. They looked upon them as exceptions to the general rule calling for the restriction of all doubtful rescripts contrary to the law. By using the phrase "*in commodum privatorum*" when speaking of rescripts contrary to the law, the legislator of the Code avoids mentioning them. They are still valid, however, as examples of rescripts that favor the public good rather than private persons. Therefore, not subject to the special norm of interpretation under consideration in this section are rescripts that are opposed to the law in favor of the public welfare or the good of religion. Included within this category of rescripts are those that are granted in favor of divine worship, the welfare of souls, and the common good of religion in general; those that benefit the common good

---

[79] Cf. *supra,* p. 130.

of society; those that grant favors to special classes, such as religious orders, clerics in general, or military personnel. Some pre-Code authors include also rescripts that grant favors to churches, monasteries, hospitals and the like.[80]

Although the above mentioned rescripts contain favors that are contrary to the prescriptions of the law, they tend to promote rather than hinder the common good. For that reason they are considered as being favorable and therefore subject to a broad interpretation. The protection afforded the common good by the law is weakened to some extent, but the harm that results is offset by the good that is done.[81]

Canon 50 speaks only of rescripts that are opposed to the *law.* In view of the teaching of pre-Code authors as noted previously, it would seem that a strict interpretation is still to be given to doubtful rescripts that are contrary to a particular statute or custom.[82] Statute is manifestly included in the term "law." According to canon 46, such rescripts, even though granted *motu proprio,* are not to be sustained unless an express derogatory clause is appended to the rescript. When such a clause is inserted, and the terms of the rescript remain doubtful, a strict interpretation must be given. When the legitimate custom or statute itself is contrary to the common law, and the rescript contains provisions that restore the force of the law, then it should be broadly interpreted whether or not the derogatory clause is inserted.[83]

Rescripts granting privileges contrary to the law are subject to the same special norms of interpretation as rescripts in general, with one exception.[84] According to canon 68 a privilege is always to be interpreted in such a way that the beneficiary will derive some benefit from the good will of the grantor.[85] Hence, no inter-

---

[80] Cf. *supra,* p. 132; Michiels, *op. cit.,* II, 431; Van Hove, *De Rescriptis,* n. 230.

[81] Michiels, *op. cit.,* II, 432.

[82] Cf. *supra,* p. 133; Van Hove, *De Rescriptis,* p. 214, note n. 4.

[83] Cf. Van Hove, *loc. cit; De Privilegiis, De Dispensationibus,* n. 205.

[84] Cans. 50 and 68 in virtue of Can. 62.

[85] "In dubio privilegia interpretanda sunt ad normam can. 50; sed ea semper adhibenda interpretatio, ut privilegio aucti aliquam ex indulgentia concedentis videantur gratiam consecuti."

pretation of the terms of a doubtful privilege is lawful unless some concession is admitted. Although a doubtful rescript granting a privilege contrary to the law *in commodum privatorum* is ordinarily subject to strict interpretation, the interpretation must not be such that the privilege will be useless.

Rescripts that grant dispensations are also subject to the special norms of canon 50.[86] While all dispensations are contrary to the law, not all of them are subject to strict interpretation. In doubt, only those dispensations are to be strictly interpreted that pertain to one or the other of the four categories of rescripts mentioned in canon 50. It should be noted, then, that dispensations that favor the common good rather than private persons are subject to a broad interpretation.

While a dispensation may receive a broad interpretation, the faculty to dispense in a certain case is always subject to strict interpretation.[87] In practice, such a faculty amounts to a dispensation *in commodum privatorum*. It is limited to one act in favor of one or more specified persons.[88] A rescript containing such a faculty must always be strictly interpreted.[89] A different norm, however, prevails in regard to rescripts that contain habitual faculties that are granted either permanently, or for a definite period of time, or for a certain number of cases. Faculties of this sort are considered to be privileges outside the law.[90] Hence, they are subject to a broad interpretation as determined by canons 50, 62 and 68.

Section 4. Rescripts Obtained for the Purpose of Acquiring an Ecclesiastical Benefice

Canon 50 mentions a fourth category of rescripts that are subject to strict interpretation in case of doubt. Included within this

---

[86] Cans. 50, 62 and 85.

[87] Can. 85.

[88] Cf. Reiffenstuel, *op. cit.*, lib. I, tit. III, n. 452; Schmalzgrueber, *op. cit.*, lib. I, tit. III, n. 30; Cicognani, *Canon Law*, pp. 857, 858; Michiels, *op. cit.*. II, 761, 762.

[89] Cans. 50, 62 and 85.

[90] Can. 66, § 1.

category are rescripts that are obtained for the purpose of acquiring an ecclesiastical benefice. The canon does not state that, in doubt, all rescripts that pertain to ecclesiastical benefices are to be strictly interpreted, but only those that are granted in order that a person might obtain such a benefice. This special norm for the interpretation of rescripts is an old one that is found in a decretal of Pope Boniface VIII, in which the Pontiff wrote:

> Although the broadest interpretation should otherwise be made in the matter of benefices, nevertheless, rescripts obtained in order that a person might acquire a benefice ought to be restricted, since they are solicited rescripts.[91]

In the section of the letter quoted above, Boniface VIII gives two norms for the interpretation of rescripts pertaining to ecclesiastical benefices. The first norm directs that rescripts of this type should ordinarily receive a broad interpretation. By way of exception, the second norm ordains that, when a rescript has been obtained for the purpose of acquiring an ecclesiastical benefice, a strict rather than a broad interpretation should be given.

Boniface gives the reason why the second norm should be used. According to him, rescripts granted in order that a person might obtain possession of an ecclesiastical benefice are solicited rescripts. He uses the term *"ambitiosae"* (*litterae*). What he means is that rescripts of this type are usually eagerly sought after. They reflect an ambitious desire on the part of those who petition them. For that reason, they should be restricted as something unfavorable.[92]

Both norms proposed by Boniface VIII for the interpretation of rescripts that have to do with ecclesiastical benefices have been retained in the present legislation of the Code. The norm calling for the strict interpretation of rescripts that concern the attain-

---

[91] C. 4, *de praebendis et dignitatibus,* III, 4 in VI. It should be noted that, according to pre-Code usage, the term *"beneficium"* had a variety of meanings. Taken in its widest sense, it meant a favor or "a benevolent action occasioning joy to its recipient."—cf. *supra,* p. 39, note n. 23. From the context of his letter, it is evident that Boniface is speaking of an ecclesiastical benefice in the sense of Canon 1409.

[92] Cf. *Glossa ordinaria* ad c. 4, *de praebendis et dignitatibus,* III, 4 in VI, s.v. *Casus.*

ment of an ecclesiastical benefice is repeated almost verbatim in canon 50.[93] The same canon directs that, in doubt, all other rescripts are to receive a broad interpretation unless they refer to litigation, are adverse to the acquired rights of others or are opposed to the law in favor of a private person. According to Boniface, rescripts that have to do with ecclesiastical benefices should ordinarily be given a broad interpretation. Canon 50 does not mention this norm as such. It is understood, however, since the canon gives a taxative enumeration of rescripts subject to strict interpretation and concludes by stating that all other rescripts are to be broadly interpreted. Unless a rescript involving an ecclesiastical benefice falls within one of the four categories of rescripts subject to strict interpretation, it is always to be given a broad interpretation whenever there is doubt as to the meaning intended in the rescript.

Of immediate interest in this section are rescripts obtained for the purpose of acquiring an ecclesiastical benefice. Boniface VIII was aware of the fact that a request for a benefice is often motivated by ambition. It was for this reason that he ordered rescripts granted in answer to such a petition to be restricted. Authors before and after the Code gave additional reasons why they should be strictly interpreted. Thus, they mention the fact that requests for a benefice often prove annoying and irksome to the grantor, due to the importunity and indiscreetness of the petitioner.[94] In addition, those who fail to receive the benefice will very often be offended.[95] Michiels adds another reason. According to him, rescripts granted for the purpose of acquiring an ecclesiastical benefice not infrequently derogate from the right of those who normally possess the power to confer the benefice.[96] This is a valid reason, but it can be reduced to the third category of canon 50, which has to do with rescripts that are opposed to the law in favor of private persons.[97]

---

[93] "In dubio, rescripta quae . . . impetrata fuerunt ad beneficii ecclesiastici assecutionem, strictam interpretationem recipiunt."

[94] Reiffenstuel, *Jus Canonicum Universum,* lib. I, tit. III, n. 128; Cicognani, Canon Law, p. 739.

[95] Cicognani, *loc. cit.;* Michiels, *Normae Generales,* II, 432.

[96] *Loc. cit.;* cf. Fagnanus, *Commentaria,* lib. V, tit. XL, c. 16, n. 30.

[97] Cf. Roelker, "An Important Rule of Law," *The Jurist,* XVII, 22.

In doubt, not all rescripts that concern the acquisition of an ecclesiastical benefice are to receive a strict interpretation. An exception is made in favor of rescripts of this kind that are granted *motu proprio.* This exception is specifically mentioned in a decretal of Pope Boniface VIII in which he distinguishes between benefices that are granted *motu proprio* and those that are granted *ad instantiam* or *ad preces.*[98] According to Boniface, if a rescript obtained for the purpose of acquiring an ecclesiastical benefice is granted *motu proprio,* then it is to be given a very broad interpretation. If it is *"ad petitionem alterius,"* then it must be strictly interpreted.

Although canon 50 makes no mention of *motu proprio* rescripts, it would seem that the norm proposed by Boniface is still valid. It is repeated among pre-Code authors as one of the norms for the interpretation of rescripts that pertain to the attainment of an ecclesiastical benefice.[99] As far as rescripts for the acquisition of benefices are concerned, the Code states that, in doubt, they are to be strictly interpreted. As part of the legislation of canon 50, this norm is taken directly from pre-Code law. Therefore, according to canon 6, § 2, it should be interpreted upon the authority of the old law and in keeping with the interpretations given by approved pre-Code authors. According to the rule laid down by Boniface VIII and repeated by pre-Code canonists, *motu proprio* rescripts obtained for the purpose of acquiring an ecclesiastical benefice are to receive a broad rather than a strict interpretation. This rule must be taken as an exception to be understood in the law of canon 50, as it was in pre-Code law. The principle is still applicable as a norm for the interpretation of rescripts. It must always be understood, however, in the light of canon 46.

---

[98] C. 24, *de praebendis et dignitatibus,* III, 4 in VI.

[99] Felinus, *Commentaria,* lib. I, tit. III, c. 18, n. 7; Pirhing, *Jus Canonicum.* lib. I, tit. III, n. 27; Schmalzgrueber, *Jus Ecclesiasticum Universum,* lib. I, tit. III, n. 27.

CHAPTER VII

The Broad Interpretation of Rescripts

The present law regulating the broad interpretation of rescripts could hardly be more simply stated than it is in canon 50. After enumerating the four types of doubtful rescripts that are subject to strict interpretation, the canon ends by stating that all others are to receive a broad interpretation. The meaning of the canon is clear. In doubt, all rescripts are to be broadly interpreted unless: 1) they refer to litigation; 2) are adverse to the acquired rights of others; 3) are opposed to the law in favor of private persons; or 4) are obtained for the purpose of acquiring an ecclesiastical benefice.

In canon 50 the legislator makes no attempt to list the various rescripts that are subject to broad interpretation. Such an enumeration would actually be superfluous. The four categories of rescripts mentioned previously in the canon embrace all the various types of rescripts that are subject to strict interpretation in case of doubt. The legislator has determined once and for all which doubtful rescripts are to be strictly interpreted. The enumeration in the canon is taxative, i.e., restricted to the items mentioned in it.[1] The very wording of the canon indicates that such is the intention of the legislator. By stating that all other rescripts are to receive a broad interpretation, he evidently means to exclude from this norm only the four categories of rescripts specifically mentioned as being subject to strict interpretation. By giving a taxative enumeration of rescripts that are to be strictly interpreted in case of doubt, he has eliminated the need for mentioning by name those that should be given a broad interpretation.

As noted in the previous chapter, the approach used by the legislator in formulating the norm for the broad interpretation of rescripts differs from that used by pre-Code canonists.[2] In

---

[1] Cf. Ojetti, *Commentarium,* I, 249; Michiels, *Normae Generales,* II, 432.

[2] Cf. *supra,* pp. 111-114.

using the rule: *"Odia restringi et favores convenit ampliari"* as a norm for the interpretation of doubtful rescripts, they attempted to distinguish between favorable and unfavorable rescripts; between those subject to strict interpretation and those subject to broad interpretation. They make specific mention of several types of rescripts which they considered to be favorable and therefore subject to broad interpretation whenever doubtful. They mention, in particular, rescripts granting what they referred to as a *purum beneficium* or *beneficium* in the strict sense. They defined a *purum beneficium* as a favor that is not contrary to the law nor injurious to the rights of others. They considered a rescript granting such a favor to be *maxime favorabile.*[3] Among other favorable rescripts, pre-Code authors make mention especially of those that are granted in behalf of divine worship, the salvation of souls, pious causes and the public welfare, as well as *motu proprio* rescripts.[4]

In canon 50, the legislator of the Code purposely avoids the use of the terms "odious" and "favorable" in regard to the rescripts that are to receive a strict or broad interpretation. By listing the only four types of rescripts that are to be strictly interpreted in case of doubt, he is able to close the canon with the brief directive that all other are to receive a broad interpretation. All the various favorable rescripts mentioned by pre-Code authors are included in this norm.

The four categories of rescripts subject to strict interpretation may be looked upon as exceptions to the norm calling for the broad interpretation of doubtful rescripts.[5] When the terms of a rescript remain doubtful, a broad or liberal interpretation will ordinarily be allowed. In general, a rescript implies a concession on the part of the superior who grants it.[6] It is entirely reasonable to expect that the benevolence of the superior extends to the full limit of his concession. In doubt, then, a broad interpretation will usually be in order. The only exceptions to this rule are the four

---

[3] Cf. Suarez, *De Legibus,* lib. VIII, c. 27, n. 2; Reiffenstuel, *Jus Canonicum Universum,* lib. I, tit. III, n. 127; cf. *supra,* p. 113.

[4] Cf. *supra,* pp. 130-133.

[5] Cf. Abbo-Hannan, *The Sacred Canons,* I, 81; Michiels, *op. cit.,* II, 429.

[6] Cf. Santi, *Praelectiones Juris Canonici,* lib. I, tit. III, n. 3.

types of rescripts enumerated in canon 50. The legislator has determined by law that these, and only these, four species of rescripts are to be strictly interpreted in case of doubt. The same law decrees that all other rescripts, in case of doubt, receive a broad interpretation.

A broad interpretation recognizes the scope of a rescript as extending as far as the proper meaning of the terms will allow. It understands the proper meaning of the terms of a rescript in their widest sense, so as to include all possible includable persons, cases or things within the proper meaning. It seeks to give full effect to the terms of a rescript, provided that there is no departure from their proper signification.

CONCLUSIONS

1. In formulating the definition and divisions of interpretation, some authors emphasize the proper meaning of the words, while others concentrate more on the will or intention of the legislator. This emphasis on one or the other aspect of interpretation is the chief cause of the diversity of terminology among them. [Cf. pp. 3-7; 15-31.]

2. The term "rescript" was often used by pre-Code canonists to designate but one type of rescript, namely, a written reply issued to further the observance of the law (*rescriptum secundum ius*). Rescripts contrary to the law (*contra ius*) and outside the law (*praeter ius*) were usually referred to as privileges, dispensations or favors. [Cf. pp. 35-40.]

3. The main difference between rescripts of justice and rescripts of favor is to be found in their subject matter. Rescripts of justice are concerned mainly with judicial matters, legal suits and the vindication of rights. Rescripts of favor contain dispensations, privileges, indulgences and the like. A favor can be granted in a rescript of justice as well as in a rescript of favor. [Cf. pp. 40-45.]

4. All rescripts are subject to the primary norm of interpretation, that is, an initial attempt must be made to understand every rescript according to the proper meaning of its terms. [Cf. pp. 51-54; 59-61.]

5. Common usage will usually determine the proper meaning of the terms of a rescript. If there are several proper meanings sanctioned by usage, the meaning common in the locality of the author of a rescript must be followed. The juridic proper signification which the terms of a rescript may have is to be preferred to all other proper meanings. [Cf. pp. 55-58; 61-64.]

6. The Code of Canon Law makes no express mention of secondary norms for the interpretation of rescripts. The very nature of legal interpretation, however, demands that every juridically

approved norm be employed to comprehend the meaning intended in a rescript. The use of the secondary norms is sanctioned in virtue of canon 20. [Cf. pp. 66-70.]

7. The *terminus a quo* or point of departure for extensive and restrictive interpretation in rescripts is the proper meaning of the words. [Cf. pp. 79-82.]

8. As a general rule, extensive or restrictive interpretation is forbidden in rescripts. Ordinarily one may never depart from the proper meaning of the terms so as to extend or restrict a rescript. [Cf. pp. 82-91; 98, 99.]

9. Only when it is clear from juridic principles of interpretation that the author of a rescript intends otherwise, may anyone other than the authentic interpreter depart from the proper meaning of the terms of a rescript so as to include persons, cases or things not expressed in the proper signification of the terms, or exclude persons, cases or things that should be included according to the proper signification. [Cf. pp. 91-98; 99-102.]

10. The special norms for the interpretation of rescripts cannot be used unless the text of a rescript is objectively doubtful. The objective doubt, if any, is established by the primary and secondary norms of interpretation embodied in canon 49. [Cf. pp. 107-109.]

11. The basis for the strict and broad interpretation of doubtful rescripts consists in the principles embodied in the Rule of Law: *"Odia restringi et favores convenit ampliari."* Pre-Code authors went to great lengths to distinguish between odious and favorable rescripts. In canon 50 the legislator makes no attempt to distinguish between the two types of rescripts. Instead, he furnishes a comprehensive enumeration of doubtful rescripts that are subject to strict interpretation and concludes by stating that, in case of doubt, all other rescripts are to receive a broad interpretation. [Cf. pp. 111-114; 142-144.]

12. The phrase "iura aliis quaesita" of canon 50 is to be understood as referring only to acquired rights, and not to rights in general. [Cf. pp. 117-128.]

BIBLIOGRAPHY

Sources

Acta Apostolicae Sedis, Commentarium Officiale, Romae, 1909-1929; Civitate Vaticana, 1929—

Codex Iuris Canonici Pii X Pontificis Maximi iussu digestus, Benedicti Papae XV auctoritate promulgatus, Praefatione, Fontium Annotatione et Indice Analytico-Alphabetico ab Emo Petro Card. Gasparri Auctus, Romae: Typis Polyglottis Vaticanis, 1917; reimpressio, 1934.

Codicis Iuris Canonici Fontes, cura Emi Petri Card. Gasparri editi, 9 vols., Romae (postea Civitate Vaticana): Typis Polyglottis Vaticanis, 1923-1939 (Vols. VII-IX, ed. cura et studio Emo Iustiniani Card. Serédi).

Corpus Iuris Canonici, ed. Lipsien. 2. post Aemilii Ludovici Richteri curas . . . instruxit Aemilius Friedberg, 2 vols., Lipsiae: Tauchnitz, 1879-1881. Editio anastatice repetita, Lipsiae: Tauchnitz, 1928.

Corpus Iuris Civilis, 3 vols., Vol. I, *Institutiones,* quas recognovit P. Krueger; *Digesta,* quae recognovit T. Mommsen et retractavit P. Krueger, ed. stereotypa 15; Vol. II, *Codex Iustinianus,* quem recognovit et retractavit P. Krueger, ed. stereotypa 10.; Vol. III, *Novellae Constitutiones,* ed. stereotypa 5., a R. Schoell; opus Schoellii morte interceptum absolvit G. Kroll; Berolini; apud Weidmannos, 1928-1929.

Corpus Iuris Civilis, 5 vols., Lugduni, 1553-1557.

Decretales D. Gregorii Papae IX, suae integretati una cum glossis restitutae, cum privilegio Gregorii XIII, Pont. Max., et aliorum Principum, Romae, 1582.

Decretum Gratiani emendatum et notationibus illustratum, una cum glossis, 2 vols., Romae, 1582.

Hardouin, Jean, *Acta Conciliorum et Epistolae Decretales ac Constitutiones Summorum Pontificum,* 11 vols. in 12, Parisiis, 1714-1715.

Jaffé, Philippus, *Regesta Pontificum Romanorum ab condita Ecclesia ad annum post Christum natum MCXCVIII,* ed. 2 correctam et auctam auspiciis G. Wattenbach, curaverunt S. Loewenfeld, F. Kaltenbrunner, P. Ewald, 2 vols., Lipsiae, 1885-1888.

Liber Sextus Decretalium D. Bonifacii Papae VIII, suae integritati cum Clementinis et Extravagantibus, earumque Glossis restitutis, Romae, 1582.

Potthast, Augustus, *Regesta Pontificum Romanorum inde ab anno post Christum natum MCXCVIII ad annum MCCCIV,* 2 vols., Berolini, 1874-1875.

Reference Works

Abbo, John A.-Hannan, Jerome D., *The Sacred Canons*, 2 vols., St. Louis: B. Herder Book Co., 1952.

Badii, Caesar, *Institutiones Iuris Canonici*, 3. ed., 2 vols., Florentiae, 1921, 1922.

Barbosa, Augustinus, *Collectanea Doctorum tam Veterum quam Recentiorum in Ius Pontificium Universum*, 4 vols., Lugduni, 1656.

Beste, Udalricus, *Introductio in Codicem*, 3. ed., Collegeville, Minn.; St. John's Abbey Press, 1946.

Böckhn, Placidus, *Commentarium in Jus Canonicum*, 3 vols., Salisburgi et invenitur Parisiis, 1776.

Bouscaren, T. I.-Ellis, A. C., *Canon Law, A Text and Commentary*, Milwaukee: The Bruce Publishing Co., 1946, Reprint, 1948.

Brys, Joseph, *Tractatus De Legibus*, Brugis: Car. Beyaert, 1942.

Buckland, William W., *A Textbook of Roman Law*, 2. ed., Cambridge: University Press, 1932.

Cappello, Felix, *Summa Iuris Canonici*, 4. ed., 3 vols., Romae: Ades Universitatis Gregorianae, 1945-1955.

Cicognani, Amleto G., *Canon Law*, 2. ed., authorized English version by Joseph M. O'Hara and Francis J. Brennan, Philadelphia: The Dolphin Press, 1935.

Cocchi, Guidus, *Commentarium in Codicem iuris canonici ad usum scholarum*, 4. ed., 8 vols., Taurinorum Augustae: Marietti, 1931-1946. Vol. I, 6. ed., 1938.

Coronata, Matthaeus Conte a, *Institutiones Iuris Canonici*, 5 vols., Taurini-Romae: Marietti, 1947-1951, Vol. I, 4. ed., 1950.

De Angelis, Philippus, *Praelectiones Juris Canonici*, 5 vols. in 9, Romae-Parisiis, 1877-1891.

De Baysio, Guido, *Rosarium seu in Decretorum Volumen Commentaria*, Venetiis, 1577.

Decius, Philippus, *Super Decretalibus*, Lugduni, 1559.

Durandus, Gulielmus, *Speculum Iuris*, Venetiis, 1577.

Engel, Ludovicus, *Collegium Universi Iuris Canonici*, 9. ed. a Caspare Barthel, Beneventi, 1760.

Fagnanus, Prosperus, *Commentaria super Quinque Libros Decretalium*, 5 vols. in 4, Venetiis, 1709.

Felinus Sandeus, *Commentaria in V Libros Decretalium*, 3 vols., Venetiis, 1570.

Ferraris, Lucius, *Prompta Bibliotheca Canonica, Iuridica, Moralis, Theologica, necnon Ascetica, Polemica, Rubrisistica, Historica*, ed. novissima, 9 vols., Romae, 1885-1899.

Gonzales-Tellez, Emmanuel, *Commentaria Perpetua in singulos Textus quinque Librorum Decretalium*, 5 vols., Lugduni, 1673.

Grandclaude, E., *Jus Canonicum juxta Ordinem Decretalium*, 5 vols. in 3, Parisiis, 1882, 1883.

Hostiensis, Cardinalis (Henricus de Segusio), *Commentaria in Quinque Decretalium Libros,* 6 vols. in 4, Venetiis, 1581.

———, *Summa Aurea,* Lugduni, 1568.

Innocentius IV, *In V Libros Decretalium Commentaria,* Venetiis, 1570.

Laymann, Paulus, *Theologia Moralis,* Venetiis, 1630.

Leurenius, Petrus, *Forum Ecclesiasticum in quo Jus Canonicum Universum Librorum ac Titulorum ordine explanatur,* 5 vols. in 3, Venetiis, 1729.

Maroto, Philippus, *Institutiones Iuris Canonici,* 2 vols., Madrid, 1919.

Michiels, Gommarus, *Normae Generales Juris Canonici,* 2. ed., 2 vols., Parisiis-Tornaci-Romae: Desclée et Socii, 1949.

Ojetti, Benedictus, *Commentarium in Codicem Iuris Canonici,* 4 vols., Romae: Apud Aedes Universitatis Gregorianae, 1927-1931.

O'Neill, William H., *Papal Rescripts of Favor,* The Catholic University of America Canon Law Studies, n. 57, Washington, D. C.: The Catholic University of America, 1930.

Panormitanus, Abbas (Nicholaus de Tudeschis), *Commentaria in Quinquc Libros Decretalium,* 5 vols. in 7, Venetiis, 1588.

Pirhing, Ernricus, *Jus Canonicum in V Libros Decretalium,* 5 vols. in 4, Dilingae, 1722.

Raymond of Peñafort, St., *Opera Omnia,* Curante Rmo. Dre. Josepho Reus et Serra, Barchinonae, 1945- , I, *Summa Iuris.*

———, *Summa Iuris,* Barcelona, 1945.

Regatillo, Eduardus, *Institutiones Iuris Canonici,* 2. ed., 2 vols., Santander: Sal Terrae, 1946.

Reiffenstuel, Anacletus, *Jus Canonicum Universum,* 5 vols. in 7, Parisiis, 1864-1870.

———, *Tractatus de Regulis Juris,* Romae, 1834.

Rigantius, Joannes, *Commentaria in Regulas, Constitutiones et Ordinationes Cancellariae Apostolicae,* 4 vols. in 2, Coloniae Allobrogum, 1751.

Roelker, Edward G., *Principles of Privilege according to the Code of Canon Law,* The Catholic University of America Canon Law Studies, n. 35, Washington, D. C.: The Catholic University of America, 1926.

Sanchez, Thomas, *De Sancti Matrimonii Sacramento Disputationum Libri Decem,* 3 vols., Venetiis, 1726.

Santi, Franciscus, *Praelectiones Juris Canonici,* 2. ed., 5 vols. in 2, Ratisbonae, Neo Eboraci et Cincinnatii, 1892.

Schmalzgrueber, Franciscus, *Jus Ecclesiasticum Universum,* 5 vols. in 12, Romae, 1843-1845.

Schmidt, John Rogg, *The Principles of Authentic Interpretation in Canon 17 of the Code of Canon Law,* The Catholic University of America Canon Law Studies, n. 141, Washington, D. C.: The Catholic University of America Press, 1941.

Suarez, Franciscus, *Opera Omnia,* 26 vols. in 28, editio nova a Carolo Berton, Paris: Apud Ludovicum Vives, 1856-1868, Tom. V, VI, *De Legibus ac Deo Legislatore, Libri Decem.*

Tuschus, Dominicus, *Practicae Conclusiones Iuris in omni foro frequentiores,* 5 vols., Lugduni, 1634.

Toso, Albertus, *Commentaria Minora ad Codicem Iuris Canonici,* 5 vols., Taurini-Romae, 1920-1927.

Van Hove, Alphonsus, *Commentarium Lovaniense,* Vol. I, Tom. II, *De Legibus Ecclesiasticis;* Tom. IV, *De Rescriptis;* Tom. V, *De Privilegiis, De Dispensationibus,* Mechliniae-Romae: H. Dessain, 1930-1939.

Vermeersch, A.-Creusen, J., *Epitome Iuris Canonici cum Commentariis ad Scholas et ad Usum Privatum,* 3 vols., Vol. I, 7. ed., 1949; Vol. II, 6. ed., 1940; Vol. III, 6. ed., 1946, Mechliniae-Romae: H. Dessain.

Wernz, Franciscus X., *Ius Decretalium,* 6 vols., Prati, Vol. I, 3. ed., 1913.

White, Porter, *The Evolution of the Canonical Concept of Strict Interpretation of Law.* Excerpta ex Dissertatione ad Lauream, Romae: Pontificia Universitas Gregoriana, 1952.

Articles

Brems, A., "De Interpretatione Authentica Codicis J. C. Per Pont. Commissionem," *Jus Pontificium,* XV (1935), 161-190, 298-313; XVI (1936), 78-105, 217-256.

Roelker, Edward, "Additional Sources in the Decretals for the Interpretation of the Law on Privileges," *The Jurist,* VII (1947), 355-377.

———, "An Important Rule of Law," *The Jurist,* XVII (1957), 9-28.

Periodicals

Jus Pontificium, Romae, 1921-1940.

Jurist, The, Washington, D. C., 1941-

ALPHABETICAL INDEX

BIOGRAPHICAL NOTE

Bernard Connor Gerhardt was born in Washington, D. C., on February 17, 1926. After graduation from Gonzaga High School in the same city in 1944, he spent two years in service with the Army Air Force. Returning to civilian life, he entered St. Charles College, Catonsville, Maryland, in the fall of 1946. He took his philosophical studies at St. Mary's Seminary, Baltimore, Maryland, and received the degree of Bachelor of Arts in 1950. From St. Mary's he went to the North American College in Rome, and while there attended the Gregorian University. He was ordained on December 19, 1953, and upon completion of his theology course was granted the Licentiate in Sacred Theology in June, 1954. After his return to the United States, he served as assistant at Holy Redeemer Church, Kensington, Maryland, until his enrollment in the School of Canon Law at the Catholic University of America, Washington, D. C., in the autumn of 1955. He received the Baccalaureate in Canon Law in June, 1956, and the degree of Licentiate in Canon Law in June, 1957.

CANON LAW STUDIES*

392. Adams, Rev. Donald E., A.B., J.C.L., The truth required in the *preces* for rescripts.
393. Bégin, Rev. Raymond F., A.B., S.T.L., J.C.L., Natural law and positive law.
394. Clancy, Rev. Walter B., A.B., J.C.L., The rites and ceremonies of sacred ordination.
395. Cox, Rev. Ronald J., S.T.L., J.C.L., A study of the juridic status of laymen in the writing of the medieval canonists.
396. Demers, Rev. Francis L., O.M.I., A.B., J.C.L., Temporal administration of the religious house in a non-exempt clerical pontifical institute.
397. Dziadosz, Rev. Henry J., M.A., S.T.L., J.C.L., The provisions of the Decree "Spiritus Sancti munera": the law for the extraordinary minister of confirmation.
398. Gerhardt, Rev. Bernard C., A.B., S.T.L., J.C.L., Interpretation of rescripts.
399. Hackett, Rev. John H., A.B., J.C.L., The concept of public order.
400. Murphy, Rev. Richard J., O.M.I., S.T.L., J.C.L., The canonico-juridical status of a communist.
401. O'Connor, Rev. David, M.S.SS.T., J.C.L., Parochial relations and co-operation of the religious and secular clergy.

*For a complete list of the available numbers of this series apply to the Catholic University of America Press, 620 Michigan Avenue, N.E., Washington (17), D. C., for a general catalogue.

www.ingramcontent.com/pod-product-compliance
Lightning Source LLC
LaVergne TN
LVHW050224080826
844660LV00012B/462

* 9 7 8 0 8 1 3 2 2 5 5 8 6 *